Joseph Alden

Elements of Intellectual Philosophy

Joseph Alden

Elements of Intellectual Philosophy

ISBN/EAN: 9783337239640

Printed in Europe, USA, Canada, Australia, Japan

Cover: Foto ©Thomas Meinert / pixelio.de

More available books at **www.hansebooks.com**

OF

INTELLECTUAL PHILOSOPHY.

BY

REV. JOSEPH ALDEN, D. D., LL. D.,

LATE PRESIDENT OF JEFFERSON COLLEGE.

NEW YORK:
D. APPLETON & CO., 90, 92 & 94 GRAND ST.
1868.

ENTERED, according to Act of Congress, in the year 1866, by
D. APPLETON & CO.,
In the Clerk's Office of the District Court of the United States for the Southern District of New York.

TO
WILLIAM CULLEN BRYANT.

As a poet you deal with reality. You have written that only which you have seen, felt, and fully believed. In preparing this elementary work on Philosophy, I have endeavored to pursue a similar course. I take great pleasure in dedicating it to one whose friendship I have long regarded as among the highest honors of my life.

JOSEPH ALDEN.

CONTENTS.

CHAPTER I.

INTRODUCTORY REMARKS, ... 13

CHAPTER II.

THE MIND'S COGNIZING POWER—FACULTIES—MENTAL ANALYSIS, ... 19

CHAPTER III.

OBJECT OF A TEXT-BOOK—METAPHORICAL LANGUAGE IN RELATION TO MENTAL OPERATIONS, . . . 25

CHAPTER IV.

COGNITION OF MATERIAL OBJECTS, ... 31

CHAPTER V.

EXTENSION—FIGURE—ORIGINAL AND ACQUIRED PERCEPTION, 37

CHAPTER VI.

Primary and Secondary Qualities of Matter, . . 44

CHAPTER VII.

Theories of Perception—Locke—Berkeley, . . 48

CHAPTER VIII.

Theories of Perception—Reid—Brown, . . . 55

CHAPTER IX.

Theory of Sir William Hamilton, . . . 63

CHAPTER X.

Relativity of Knowledge, ... 71

CHAPTER XI.

Remarks on the Nature of Perception, . . . 80

CHAPTER XII.

Cognition of Mental Operations—Personality—Unity—Identity—Consciousness, ... 84

CHAPTER XIII.

Cognition of Space, ... 100

CHAPTER XIV.

Cognition of Time, ... 107

CHAPTER XV.

COGNITION OF RELATIONS, ... 111

CHAPTER XVI.

RESEMBLANCE AND GENERALIZATION—GENERAL AND ABSTRACT
TERMS, ... 115

CHAPTER XVII.

CAUSE AND EFFECT, ... 128

CHAPTER XVIII.

COGNITION OF BEAUTY, ... 147

CHAPTER XIX.

COGNITION OF RECTITUDE, ... 163

CHAPTER XX.

REASONING, ... 189

CHAPTER XXI.

MATHEMATICAL REASONING, ... 203

CHAPTER XXII.

THE SYLLOGISM, ... 215

CHAPTER XXIII.

MEMORY, ... 223

CHAPTER XXIV.

Association, ... 240

CHAPTER XXV.

Imagination, ... 248

CHAPTER XXVI.

The Will, ... 261

CHAPTER XXVII.

Attention, ... 280

CHAPTER XXVIII.

Understanding and Reason—Faith—Infinity, . . 284

PREFACE.

THE object of this book is not to teach a system of philosophy, but to aid the student in studying subjects which are adapted to promote fixedness of attention and discrimination of thought, and which underlie all thinking pertaining to human action and progress. This object has determined the selection of topics, and the mode of treating them. The topics treated relate chiefly to the cognitive faculties. The general plan is indicated by the following questions: *What can the mind do? How does it do it?*

The book might well enough be termed "Elementary Exercises in Thinking." In an experience of more than a quarter of a century as a college teacher, the author found that he was successful just in proportion as he was elementary in his instructions. If men become familiar with the alphabet of thinking, they are prepared for progress toward profoundness.

In accordance with the object above stated, no topic has received an exhaustive discussion; and yet no topic has received superficial consideration. The first books put into the hands of the student should not be commonplace compilations, but should be characterized by a freshness, vivacity, and clearness of thought which may be communicated to his mind. This will be of more value than numberless propositions committed to memory.

The book may be found serviceable to those desirous of improvement who may not be favored with a teacher. They will find no difficulty in understanding it. The author believes that there is nothing cognizable in philosophy which cannot be clearly expressed in good English; though, as Dr. Chalmers remarks, he "is fully aware that whosoever, in treating of the human mind, aims to be understood, must lay his account with forfeiting, in the opinion of a very large proportion of his readers, all pretensions to depth, to subtlety, and to invention."

The author has no desire to inspire a love of metaphysical disputation, or of metaphysical lore. The object of education is to fit men for the service of God here and hereafter. Life here is for wise action. Habits of sober and accurate thought are among the conditions of wise action. Such habits the study of philosophy should form.

The teacher whose views of the end and method of teaching correspond with those of the author, will find the book abundantly large enough for the length of time usually devoted to this study in our schools and colleges. The college teacher who may see fit to use it, may find that his discussions with his pupils in connection with the text, will prepare them to understand and appreciate the supplementary lectures which he will doubtless feel inclined to prepare.

Should the work meet the approbation of teachers, and be used as a text-book to a considerable extent, it is the intention of the author to prepare, for the benefit of those who have entered upon a course in philosophy under his guidance, a volume embracing additional topics and more extended investigations.

J. A.

ELEMENTS

OF

INTELLECTUAL PHILOSOPHY.

CHAPTER I.

INTRODUCTORY REMARKS.

NUMEROUS definitions of philosophy have been given. It would be of no advantage to repeat them. We have before us a field to explore. It is of comparatively little importance what name we give to the field, or to the process of exploration.

A perfect definition of a science must include all that belongs to it, and exclude all that does not belong to it. It marks, therefore, the completion, not the commencement of the science.

When used with reference to investigations which have the mind for their subject, the term philosophy is synonymous with science. Mental philosophy and mental science are the same.

Mental philosophy has the mind for its subject-matter; just as natural philosophy has the material world for its subject-matter.

The mind is a spiritual existence which perceives, remembers, imagines, loves, etc.; that is, which performs operations which we call perceiving, remembering, imagining, loving.

Existence cannot be defined. There is no such thing as existence, apart from things existing. Every one knows what it is for a thing to be—to exist. To the questions, What is being? In what does existence consist? no answers conveying information can be given.

The mind is a spiritual existence. By spiritual is meant that which is not material—the antithesis of material. We describe the mind positively, when we state what it can do. We describe it negatively, when we state that it has none of the qualities of matter.

The mind is self-active, and can think, feel, and will. Matter is inert, extended, and divisible. Objects with qualities so different cannot reasonably be regarded as identical.

We know the mind as connected with the body. Its action is modified by the body. The acts which we term mental acts are the acts of mind connected with a material organization. What acts a disembodied mind can perform, we do not know. Our knowledge is confined to acts of mind united to the body.

A mental act may be conditioned on a state of the body; but it is, nevertheless, an act of the mind. An act of perception may be conditioned on the state of the brain; but the brain without the mind cannot perform an act of perception. The act is therefore a mental act. A pain felt in the finger is felt by the mind; for, if the mind be taken away, no laceration of the finger will occasion pain.

The first thing to be done in studying the science of mind, is to observe the operations of the mind. The mind can observe its own operations. It can make its own operations the object of attention, just as it can make the operations of a sewing-machine the object of attention.

The mind sees the operations of the machine through the instrumentality of the eyes. It sees its own operations by a direct beholding. The question, "How can the mind cognize its own operations?" is as easily answered as the question, "How can the mind cognize the operations of a machine?"

It is sometimes said that we cognize our mental acts by means of consciousness—as though consciousness were an instrument by which we cognize them.

We must be careful to avoid mistaking words for things—imaginary processes for real processes. To say that we cognize our mental operations by means of consciousness, is simply to say that we do cognize them. To say that consciousness informs us of what takes place in our minds, is simply to say that the mind cognizes its own operations. Such forms of expression do not explain how the cognition takes place.

Some writers have used language which would seem to imply that a definite act or operation of consciousness is necessary to make known to us each thought and feeling; that without the putting forth of such an act, our thoughts and feelings would be unknown to us. A writer says, "Consciousness is the faculty by which the various powers of the mind are made known to us." If by this he means to assert that the mind must put forth action in order that we may know what powers of action it possesses, the assertion is true; but if he means to assert that a separate and peculiar act of consciousness is necessary to make known to us our mental acts, just as an act of perception is necssary to make known to us the existence of external objects, the assertion is not true. It lacks proof. It leads to an absurdity.

We have a mental act—an act of memory, we will suppose. According to the theory above stated, an act of consciousness is necessary to make known to us that act of memory. This act of consciousness, being a mental act, must needs have another act of consciousness to make it known to us, and that another, and so on *ad infinitum!*

This erroneous view is the result of supposing that there is an analogy between the mode by which the mind cognizes external objects, and the mode by which it cognizes its own operations. False analogies and imaginary mental processes are frequent sources of error.

Accurate observation of our mental operations is difficult. The habit of observation can be formed by earnest and patient effort. No progress can be made in the study of mind, unless this habit be formed. The operations of the mind, the facts which are the subjects of study, must, in every instance, be observed by the student for himself. Facts recorded by others will be of no service to him, except as they enable him to see them for himself. "Instruction can do little more than point out the position in which the pupil ought to place himself, in order to verify, by his own experience, the facts which his instructor proposes to him as true." The pupil may "get by heart" systems of philosophy (so called); but little or no benefit will result beyond that of improving a verbal memory.

It may be a useful exercise for the young student to reverse his train of thought. Let him observe what thought now occupies his mind; then let him endeavor to recall the thought which immediately preceded it, and so on, as far as recollection will enable him to go. He will thus be aided in making his mental acts the object of attention.

Let the pupil, at the outset, resolve to be satisfied with nothing short of clear definite ideas in relation to the subject considered. Earnest and steady looking at a subject, will render that clear which at first appears confused and obscure, or will enable him to decide that there are no materials for positive definite knowledge before him. Let the line between what he sees, and what he does not see, be clearly drawn.

CHAPTER II.

THE MIND'S COGNIZING POWER—FACULTIES—MENTAL ANALYSIS.

THE mind has capacities for action. It can do various things. It can know, it can feel, it can will.

It can perform different acts of knowing, that is, it can acquire different kinds of knowledge, and can acquire knowledge under different conditions. It can cognize the existence and qualities of matter. It can cognize the relations between geometrical figures. It can cognize, to some extent, the causes of events. It can cognize the difference between right and wrong. These different acts of the mind are distinguishable, and can be classified. We can form classes of mental acts.

These classes exist as classes in our minds only. As our mental operations actually take place, those belonging to different classes are blended. The successive mental acts of an hour may include examples from all the classes formed. The mind does not perform one class of acts exclusively for a time, and then pass to the performance of acts of another class.

Acts of a particular class may predominate at a given time, but various other acts are interspersed with them, or are contemporaneous.

A man may be viewing a landscape. He is earnestly engaged in cognizing its different points of interest—the hill, the stream, the grove, the cottage. Perceptions constitute the majority of his mental acts, but other acts intervene. He remembers having seen similar objects: he infers that the occupant of the cottage must be a man of taste. Recollections and inferences are thus blended with his perceptions.

Mental acts are classified on the principle of resemblance. The resemblance has reference to the objects acted upon by the mind.

We can look upon the different operations of a machine, and can compare the operations, as well as the results produced. Not so with the mind. The acts of the mind, regarded as analogous to the revolution of the wheels of a machine, are invisible—incognizable. We cannot see *how* the mind perceives: we see that it does perceive, and what it perceives. We can compare mental operations in their results only.

In view of the different objects which the mind can act upon—in view of the different things which the mind can do, we can classify its operations, and ascribe the operations thus classified to different faculties.

A faculty is not a component part of the mind. The mind is not made up of faculties as its constituent parts. When the mind is cognizing external objects, we say it is exercising the faculty of perception. When it is recalling past thoughts, we say it is exercising the faculty of memory. When it is cognizing a truth by the aid of other truths, we say it is exercising the faculty of reasoning. We use the term faculty to express the different modes of the mind's action. We must remember that it is the mind which perceives, remembers, reasons; not something separate from it termed a faculty. A faculty denotes a power of the mind to act in a particular way.

We may regard the mind as having a greater or smaller number of faculties, according as we form a greater or smaller number of classes of mental operations. We may form a greater or smaller number of classes, according as we pass by or notice minor differences in the objects acted upon by the mind.

The mind can cognize truth. We say it has a faculty for cognizing truth. It can cognize different kinds of truth. It can cognize truth relating to material objects. It can cognize truth relating to human duty. It can cognize truth relating to space and numbers. We may thus form three classes of truths, viz., material, moral, and mathematical. We may thus ascribe to the mind three cognitive faculties.

We may carry our classification still further, and

speak of a greater number of cognitive faculties, and speak in accordance with the truth. We may ascribe to the mind a greater or smaller number of faculties, and may state nothing but truth in so doing. The question before the student is not, how many faculties has the mind, but what operations can it perform? In determining this question, it is convenient for us to classify the operations we observe. We need to form classes enough to include all the operations of the mind. There may be a needless yet truthful multiplication of classes, and, consequently, of faculties. Let it be remembered that the term faculty is used simply to denote a particular mode of the mind's action.

It has been said, that the method to be pursued in the study of mental philosophy is the same as in natural philosophy, viz., to observe facts, and infer principles or laws. The remark requires some modification, in consequence of the difference in the materials composing the two sciences. The instrument by which both are studied is the same; but the subjects differ. The one is inert matter; the other is self-active mind. In both cases we are to observe facts; but in the one case we ask, What are the passive phenomena before us, and to what laws are they subject? In the other case we ask, What can the mind do? The difference does not relate so much to method, as to the attitude of mind. There is some advantage in viewing the mental phenomena as the acts of a voluntary being, instead of viewing them as succeeding each other according to certain laws.

The student must form the habit of analyzing his mental operations.

To analyze a chemical substance, is to resolve it into its constituent elements. A simple substance cannot be analyzed. To analyze a mental process, is to separate, in thought, the different mental acts which constitute that process. A simple mental act cannot be analyzed.

The mind is seldom in a simple state; that is, is seldom employed in performing a simple act. It is seldom that one simple thought is present to the mind to the exclusion of all other thoughts. To notice separately the different acts or states which constitute a given complex state, is to analyze that complex state.

One is looking upon a meadow. The state of his mind is that of perception. There are various objects before him — grass, lilies, trees, cattle. He hears the songs of the birds, and the murmur of the rivulet by which he is standing. The state of his mind is complex, and consists of various perceptions by means of the eye and the ear. To notice them separately in thought, is to analyze that complex state.

The habit of analyzing our mental states is adapted to promote nice discrimination. Skill in distinguishing between nice shades of color is desirable; but skill in distinguishing between nice shades of thought is still more desirable. He who would become an acute thinker, must train his mind to habits of mental analysis.

CHAPTER III.

OBJECT OF A TEXT-BOOK—METAPHORICAL LANGUAGE IN RELATION TO MENTAL OPERATIONS.

To view truths directly, and not through the medium of another's mind, or from a traditional standpoint, should be the object of every student. His text-book should be used as the traveller uses his guide-book.

The traveller visits Rome. He gets a guide-book, that he may know where to go, and what to see. Each morning he consults his guide-book, and by its aid forms the plans of the day. He visits St. Peter's and the Vatican, and examines the objects mentioned in his guide-book. He does not spend his time in committing to memory the descriptions contained in the book, but in seeing the objects described. When questioned respecting St. Peter's and the Vatican, he does not repeat from memory what he has read, but tells what he has seen.

So with a text-book in mental science. Its object is not to tell men what to believe, but what to see.

Unless a man becomes a *seer*, he derives no advantage from his text-book or his teacher.

The student must guard against being misled by the use of metaphorical language. Many of the terms employed to denote the operations of the mind are metaphorical. They were originally employed to express material objects and material phenomena.

We call a certain operation or state of mind, a mental image. We speak of having in our minds an image of the Capitol, or of some other remarkable edifice. In reality, there can be no resemblance between the Capitol and that state of mind—that condition of an immaterial, invisible existence—which we call having an image or picture of the Capitol in the mind. We must be on our guard, lest the use of the term image should modify our view of the state of mind to which it is applied.

We speak of a deep impression made upon the memory, and of its erasure by time. The language is metaphorical, and should not lead us to suppose that there is an analogy between an impression upon wax and an impression upon memory. And yet this assumed analogy is sometimes used to account for facts. For instance, it is a fact made known by observation and experience, that some minds remember events very easily for a time, but do not remember them long. To account for the fact, it is said that impressions easily made are easily effaced: this passes for an explanation of the fact above stated.

State the matter thus: Impressions easily made on material objects are, for the most part, easily effaced: therefore things easily committed to memory are easily forgotten. Every one sees that the conclusion does not follow from the premise.

The explanation owes its plausibility to the supposed analogy between impressions on matter and the mental act of remembering. There is no such analogy. The idea is suggested by the metaphorical use of the term impression. The student must be on his guard against being thus misled.

He must also avoid drawing literal conclusions from figurative premises. For example, conscience is said to be the voice of God in the soul: hence, its dictates must be infallibly correct.

The premise is figurative; the conclusion literal. The expression, "Conscience the voice of God in the soul," means, "God has given the soul power to cognize the difference between right and wrong—to cognize duty and its opposite." Give the premise a literal form, and the matter stands thus: God has given the mind power to cognize the difference between right and wrong; therefore all its decisions are infallible. With just as much truth it may be said, " God has given the mind power to distinguish between truth and error; therefore all its decisions are infallible."

" Although," says Sir William Drummond, " it be very difficult to speak of the mind without employing figurative language and without borrowing from analogy, yet it is altogether unphilosophical to build an argument on a trope, or found a system on a simile."

Another source of error is that resulting from personification of the faculties. The different faculties, which, we have seen, are only different modes of the mind's operation, have been treated as separate and independent personalities, having extensive dealings with one another, and with their master, the mind. This source of error has been noticed by several writers, yet few have successfully guarded against it. Some eminent modern writers have, by their excessive personification of the faculties, poured confusion over the whole mental field.

Hobbes censured "that metaphorical speech of attributing command and subjection to the faculties of the soul, as if they made a commonwealth or family within themselves, and could speak to one another."

Locke says: "I suspect that this way of speaking of faculties has led many into a confused notion of so many distinct agents within us, which had their several provinces and authorities, and did command, obey, and perform several actions as so many distinct beings; which has been no small occasion of wrangling, obscurity, and uncertainty in questions relating to them."

Notice some illustrations of the error to be avoided. "The senses inform us of the existence of the external world." The senses are here represented as intelligent agents giving information to another intelligent agent, the mind—"us." The truth intended to be conveyed is, "The mind, through the organs of sense, cognizes the external world."

"Perception furnishes the memory and reason with materials on which to act." Avoiding personification, the thought is, "The mind perceives truths, remembers them, and cognizes other truths by their aid."

"When we attend to any change which happens in nature, judgment informs us that there must be a cause of this change." Literally, "When the mind attends to any change, it perceives that the change or event must have had a cause." The language used above implies that judgment is an agent separate from the mind, whereas it is an act of the mind.

No writer has carried personification of the faculties to a greater length than has Kant. "Pure reason," he says, "leaves every thing to the understanding which refers immediately to the objects of the intuition, or rather to their synthesis in the imagination." Here the mind disappears altogether, and certain imaginary entities take its place.

"The understanding cannot perceive, and the senses cannot think."

Here the faculties are represented as independent entities. Literally expressed, the thought is, "The mind cannot, except through the organism of the senses, cognize material objects, and cannot cognize spiritual objects by the said organism of the senses."

Cousin says: "The senses attest the existence of concrete quantities and bodies; consciousness, the internal sense, attests the presence of a succession of thoughts, and of all the phenomena which pertain to personal identity; but at the same time reason intervenes, and pronounces that the relations of the quantities in question are abstract, universal, and necessary."

The senses, consciousness, and reason, are here set forth as personages doing the work of the mind. To use such language in describing the acts of the one indivisible mind, tends to produce obscurity and error.

The above illustrations show, that facts in relation to the mind "should be stated in the simplest, most direct, and least figurative language we can select." When compelled to use metaphorical terms, we should notice exactly the meaning intended to be conveyed by them.

CHAPTER IV.

COGNITION OF MATERIAL OBJECTS.

WHAT can the mind do? It can know—cognize—acquire knowledge. These forms of expression are identical.

What can the mind cognize? It can cognize matter—the external world. It cognizes matter through the senses. When it is asked, How can the mind cognize matter through the senses? we can state the conditions of cognition, and that is all we can do.

These conditions may be stated thus: An object is presented to the organ of sense. A tree, for example, is so presented that the light reflected from it enters the eye, and forms an image upon the retina, which is an expansion of the optic nerve in the back part of the eye. If the optic nerve and the brain be in a healthful state, the mind cognizes the tree—that is, perceives its existence, form, and color. Why these conditions are followed by cognitions, we do not know. God has so ordained.

If any of these conditions are wanting, cognition

will not take place. If the eye is disordered so that an image is not formed on the retina—if the optic nerve or the brain be not in their normal state, cognition will not take place.

When we have stated the conditions of cognition, we have not told how the mind cognizes. The conditions are material or physiological; the act of cognition is mental. Keeping in mind this distinction will aid us in avoiding error. The act of cognition is a simple act, and cannot be explained otherwise than by stating its conditions and results. We should never attempt to explain what is unexplainable.

We have stated the conditions of cognition by the sense of sight. In cognition by the sense of touch, the conditions are, that the object be brought in contact with the organ—the hand, for example—and that the connection formed by the nerves between the organ and the brain be uninterrupted, and that the nerves and brain be in a normal state.

In cognition by the ear, the vibrations of the air must strike upon the tympanum, and the impression or affection thereby produced be transmitted, by means of the bones of the ear and the auditory nerve, to the brain.

In cognition by taste, the object must be applied to the organ, and the impression transmitted to the brain. So in smelling.

We call the effect of the presentation of the

object to the organ, an impression. By this term we mean that change, whatever it may be, which experience has shown is necessary to cognition. The same may be said of the phrase, "transmitted by the nerves to the brain." We mean by it, that state of the nerves and brain, whatever it may be, which experience has shown is necessary to cognition.

How do we know that matter exists? We see it—feel it—cognize it. Does the eye see it? Does the hand feel it? Take away the mind, and what can the eye or the hand do? It is the mind that sees and feels. It is the mind which cognizes the existence of the tree, just as it is the mind which cognizes the relation of equality between two and two. In the one case, the agency of the senses is used; in the other, not.

If it be asked, How do we know that things are as we perceive them to be? How do we know that matter exists? we can only reply, "We know it." We cannot doubt the direct, intuitive cognitions of our minds. We cannot doubt that the whole of an object is greater than its part. We cannot doubt that the tree standing before us exists. The ground of the certainty of our knowledge is, in both cases, the same. We must accept our intuitive cognitions as true.

It is said that consciousness assures us of the truth of our cognitions. It has already been remarked, that to see an object, and to be conscious that we see an object, is one and the same thing. To ask, How do you know that you are conscious that you see an object? is to ask, How do you know that you see it?

Some say, We are conscious of the state of mind termed cognition or perception, and of nothing else. We see an external object. The seeing—cognizing, is confessedly a mental act. Of its existence, it is said, we are certain; but we are not certain of any thing else. We are not certain that there is any thing external corresponding to this state of mind, which alone is the object of consciousness. Thus we have no certainty of the existence of external objects.

The error contained in the above statement consists in not taking the whole of the conscious state of mind into view. That of which we are conscious is this: we are conscious that we cognize the object. When we say we are conscious that we have a cognition—a subjective state of mind—we have not stated the whole truth. Our consciousness embraces the cognition of the object. We are as certain that we cognize the object, as we are that we have a mental state.

The term consciousness is properly confined to our mental operations. We cannot, in strict propriety, say that we are conscious of a tree; but we can say we are conscious that we perceive a tree.

If it be asked, What is the object of the mind in perception? the reply is, The object perceived. The objects of cognition are the things cognized. If we scrutinize our mental operations, we shall find nothing but the act of mind and the objects perceived. If it be asked, How can the mind, which is spirit, act upon matter? How can the mind act upon objects at a distance from it, as in the case of perception by the eye? we reply, The mind does act on matter, so far as cognizing it is concerned, and it does cognize distant objects. In proof of this, we appeal to consciousness—that is, to observation of what takes place when we cognize external objects.

Some philosophers have labored hard to discover how the idea of externality—of something external—is first acquired. It is acquired when the mind cognizes an external object. Whenever the mind cognizes an object out of the mind, it cognizes it as out of the mind. No one, in cognizing a material object by means of sight or touch, ever cognized it as a modification of his own mind, or as existing within his mind.

Do we get the idea of something external through the agency of any of our senses except touch and sight? Take the sense of hearing. Suppose a person destitute of all the senses except hearing. Let a violin be sounded near him. What would be the effect on his mind? He would cognize a sound; and he would cognize it as external to his own mind. He would have no knowledge of the violin; but he would have a knowledge of sound. He would not have a knowledge of something external extended and offering resistance to muscular effort; but he would have a knowledge of sound as external to his mind, and could probably infer the existence of a cause external to his mind.

In like manner, we may have a knowledge of something external to us, in the exercise of all our senses. We get the idea of externality through all our senses; but not, in all cases, the idea of extended externality. A distinction is to be made between externality extended and unextended.

CHAPTER V.

EXTENSION—FIGURE—ORIGINAL AND ACQUIRED PER-
CEPTIONS.

"It is certain that sight alone, and independently of touch, affords us the idea of extension; for extension is the necessary object of vision, and we should see nothing if we did not see it extended. I even believe that sight must give us the notion of extension more readily than touch, because sight makes us remark more promptly and permanently than touch that contiguity, and, at the same time, that distinction of parts in which extension consists. Moreover, vision alone gives us the idea of the color of objects. Let us suppose now parts of space differently colored and presented to our eyes. The difference of colors will necessarily cause us to observe the boundaries or limits which separate two neighboring colors, and, consequently, will give us an idea of figure, for we conceive of a figure when we conceive a limitation or boundary on all sides."

An appeal to our consciousness, that is, observation of what takes place in the exercise of vision, shows that the mind cognizes extension and form by means of the eye; that is, cognizes extended and figured objects by means of the eye.

Some contend that we get the idea of extension and figure by means of the sense of touch, and that those ideas are, by association, transferred to our visual perceptions. So far is this from being clear, it is doubtful whether any accurate idea of figure could be gained by the sense of touch only. Let one be blindfolded, and then let an object different from any object previously seen and handled be presented to the sense of touch, and he will form a very inaccurate idea of its figure.

Some admit that we can cognize extension by the eye, but deny that we can cognize figure, that is, solidity, length, breadth, and thickness. That we now acquire a knowledge of solidity by the eye is, it is said, the result of inference from our experience gained by the sense of touch. It is admitted that we seem to cognize solidity by means of sight, and in reply, it is said that we seem to cognize distance by the sense of sight, whereas our cognition of distance is an inference or judgment. Now we affirm that we do cognize distance by means of the eye. Those who deny this assume that in all our primary perceptions by sight all objects appear equally near. This is a mere assumption. Memory does not reveal to us our first perceptions. The oft-quoted case of Cheselden's patient has no bearing upon the point. The imperfect cognition by means of the organ before it was in its normal state, shows nothing as to the original design of the organ. Young children have very inaccurate cognitions of the distance of objects, but they give no indications of cognizing all objects as equally near.

We cognize external objects as external. We cognize them as distinct from us, and distant from us. The *quantity* of distance is imperfectly cognized by the eye. A process of inference is added to the visual perception, and thus our cognitions become more and more accurate.

The state of mind which we call seeing distance, is a complex state. We see an object—a tower for example. We see it as distant from us. When we make the distance an object of attention, and attempt to determine the amount of the distance, a process of inference takes place. In view of a former analogous experience, the mind decides that the object is, say, five miles distant. The cognition in regard to the exact distance is not a direct cognition. It is an inference or judgment founded upon the visual appearance of the object, conjoined with former experience. In many instances, this process of inferring is so rapid that it escapes our attention.

It is asked, How, since the image on the retina is inverted, do we see objects upright? The reply is, we do see them upright. This we know. Why the physical conditions of perception are as they are, we do not know. A similar answer may be given to the question, why, when there is an image of the object in each eye, we see but one object. Some recent discoveries in optics reveal in a measure the connection between binocular vision and the cognition of form.

A distinction exists between our original and our acquired perceptions. The one class are perceptions proper, the other inferences. The distinction may also be expressed by calling the former direct cognitions, and the latter indirect cognitions.

We hear music: we say we hear a hand-organ in the street. In truth, we hear the sounds produced by the organ. By means of sight or touch, we have cognized the existence of organs. We have learned that a particular instrument is the cause of particular sounds. When we cognize those sounds, we seem to cognize the instrument. But the mental process is as follows. We hear the sound, and infer the presence of an organ. The inference is founded on our experience. On former occasions, we have known that similar sounds proceeded from an organ. On the principle that like causes produce like effects, we infer that the sounds which we now hear proceed from an organ. That there is an organ in the street is an inference from analogy.

We see a plate of butter, and we say it looks soft. But softness and hardness are not originally cognized by the eye, but by touch. We have found, from tactual examination, that butter under certain conditions is soft. We have noted the appearance it then presented. When we see that appearance, we infer softness. We do not see softness, but the signs from which we infer it. We must thus learn to distinguish between our sense perceptions and our inferences. Both are acts of the mind, but they are not identical —do not belong to the same class.

Are our perceptions copies of external objects? Does the perception of a rose resemble a rose? Is there a resemblance between the idea of a rose and the material rose?

To perceive a rose, to have an idea of a rose, is a mental act—an act of a spiritual, invisible, indivisible existence. Can there be any resemblance between said act and a rose?

That such a resemblance exists is sometimes assumed. It might be regarded as a harmless error, were it not that it may influence one's subsequent thinking. An inference may be drawn from the assumption. That inference may form a portion of an argument, which must therefore be unsound. It may well be doubted whether there can be any such thing as harmless error. It is always liable to influence our thinking.

The phrase, mental image or picture, is properly used to express a particular state of mind. We speak of having a mental picture, conception, or image of some edifice we have seen—of the church we were accustomed to frequent in our early days. A moment's reflection will show that there can be no resemblance between the church, a material object, and the act of mind calling it to distinct remembrance.

We may, from reading or hearing a description of a scene, form a conception, or image, or picture of said scene in our minds. Those terms express a certain state of mind; but that state of mind, while it has a certain relation to the material objects, has no literal resemblance to them.

It may be asked, Are all mental acts alike? Is the perception of a rose like the perception of a stone?

The act of perception cannot be distinguished in thought from the perception—that is, the perception as act cannot be distinguished from the perception as knowledge. The only difference we can perceive with respect to the acts above mentioned is, the one is the perception of a rose, the other of a stone.

Is it proper to say, "I believe in the existence of a material world"? We have seen that by the organism of the senses, we cognize the existence of the material world. To cognize a truth immediately, and to believe a truth, are different mental acts. We believe a friend's statement in regard to something he has witnessed: we believe that statement to be true, but we do not know it to be true. We know that the whole is greater than its part, and that matter exists. Our knowledge of these truths is direct, intuitive.

Belief is founded on testimony or evidence, and is clearly distinguishable from intuitive cognition.

We may have beliefs in whose truth we have as much confidence as we have in our intuitive cognitions. Still a belief is not an intuitive cognition. As our cognition of the existence of matter is intuitive, it should not be spoken of as a belief.

CHAPTER VI.

PRIMARY AND SECONDARY QUALITIES OF MATTER.

MATTER is that which possesses certain qualities. Some of these qualities are intuitively cognized; others are the subjects of inference. To the questions, What is matter apart from its qualities? What is the essence of matter? we answer, we do not know that there is any such thing.

Some of the qualities of matter are essential to its existence as matter. Some qualities are common to all matter. There are other qualities which belong to some kinds of matter only.

The division made by most writers, is that of primary and secondary. The primary qualities are those which are common to all matter. Thus extension is a primary quality.

Secondary qualities are those which belong to some kinds of matter. Thus fragrance, heat, sonorousness, belong to some kinds of matter, but not to all.

The primary qualities are cognized directly, intuitively. The cognition of them is, in fact, inseparable from the cognition of matter—is the cognition of matter. If we did not cognize matter as extended and solid, or having the capability of resisting pressure, we should not cognize it at all.

The secondary qualities are cognized indirectly. Their existence is inferred from certain effects. You see a musical instrument—a violin, for example. You cognize it as matter having extension and resistance. You do not cognize the fact that it, or certain portions of it, has the quality of producing musical sound. The strings are made to vibrate: you have a cognition of sound. From observation you conclude that the sound is produced by the vibration of the strings: you conclude those strings are possessed of a peculiar quality—a quality not possessed by all forms of matter. The cognition of this quality is not a direct, but an indirect cognition.

The same remarks may be made respecting the quality of fragrance.

With respect to flavor or taste, the case is different. Apply a sweet body to the organ, and the perception of sweetness is immediate—as immediate as the perception of extension or resistance. We are as certain that we cognize sweetness directly as that we cognize hardness directly.

The secondary qualities are affirmed by some to have no existence except in the mind. "These are not," says Hamilton, "in propriety qualities of bodies at all. As apprehended, they are only subjective affections, and belong only to bodies in so far as these are supposed to be furnished with the powers capable of specifically determining the various parts of our nervous apparatus to the particular action, or rather passion, of which they are susceptible; which determined action or passion is the quality of which we are immediately cognizant; the external concause of that internal effect remaining to the perception altogether unknown." The error of regarding the secondary qualities as existing only in the mind, has arisen from applying the same term to the mental affection and the cause of that affection. Heat, as a feeling, exists only in the mind; but heat, as a cause of that feeling, is a real quality. Let one touch a piece of red-hot iron. He will cognize the fact that the iron has heat. He may not be able to tell what it consists of, but that does not nullify his cognition of its existence. He is not able to tell what extension consists of, but that does not nullify his cognition of extension.

Sound, it is said, exists only in the mind. It is true that it exists, as a cognition, in the mind, but the cause of that cognition is as truly a quality of the violin as extension is a quality.

Color is said to be in the mind only. We see only the light, it is said. The color of an object depends upon the rays of light which it reflects. An object which reflects green rays, appears green, and one which reflects red rays, appears red. But, why does one object reflect green rays and another red? Is there not something in the object which reflects green rays—some peculiar arrangement of the particles of matter which causes the reflection of those rays? If so, then there is something in the object which determines its color, and color is not a creation of the mind.

Do we not know what color consists in, as well as we know what gravity consists in, and what extension consists in?

Is it, then, proper to speak of some qualities in matter as the unknown cause of certain mental affections? May it not just as well be said, that extension is the unknown cause of a certain mental state which we call the cognition of extension, as to say that savor is the unknown cause of a certain mental affection which we term the cognition of sweetness? In the one case, we cognize the body as extended; in the other, we cognize it as sapid.

There has been, it seems to us, an unnecessary amount of labor bestowed upon this distinction in regard to the qualities of matter. The threefold distinction of Hamilton has led to no beneficial results. The sum of what can be safely affirmed, seems to be this: Some qualities are essential to matter—belong to all matter. Some qualities belong only to certain portions of matter. In regard to these qualities (of both kinds), some are cognized directly, and some indirectly. Some are cognized more clearly than others. In short, our knowledge of the qualities of matter, like our knowledge of other subjects, is made up of intuitive perceptions and inferences.

CHAPTER VII.

THEORIES OF PERCEPTION—LOCKE—BERKELEY.

VARIOUS opinions have been held on the subject of perception. Some of them must be briefly considered.

"It is singular, and at first sight unaccountable, how it should ever have been propounded, that in the act of perception, as, for example, in looking at a tree, there is an independent image, form, or phantasm, or idea of the tree, interposed between the tree itself and the percipient being.

"A man has only to look at any object before him, not contenting himself with words, to be satisfied of the non-existence of any such image or idea. To one of untutored and unperverted mind, the very suggestion of such a thing would appear absurd. He perceives the external object, and, let him look as intently as he may, he can perceive nothing else.

"Philosophers, however, were not content with simple facts, and a simple statement of these facts.

"Amongst other conceits, divers of them appear to have entertained the notion that some intermediate image or phantasm is requisite, for the unmeaning reason, that the immaterial mind cannot come into contact with matter, or have any communication with it, except, as several of these philosophers suppose, through a fine, filmy, shadowy, unsubstantial medium; overlooking that it is the business of philosophy at all times to take facts as they are, to regard what is done,—not to perplex itself with hypothetical impossibilities. What mind can do, and what matter can do, must be determined by dry facts. The best proof of the practicability of a thing, is that it takes place.

"They might have known, by merely opening their eyes, that intelligent beings *do* see material objects, and that in this simple act they are utterly unconscious of any image, species, idea, representation, or whatever else a metaphysician might choose to call that imaginary entity.

"Even philosophers who did not consider any independent entity of this kind to exist, held the kindred doctrine that there is a purely mental phenomenon, which is the immediate thing perceived, either constituting the object itself, or intervening in some inexplicable way between the external object and the percipient being, so as practically to prevent him from getting at the object, or to keep it aloof from him; an hypothesis, in whatever way it may be put or expressed, that embodies as rank a fiction as the other.

"It seems to have been only after a thousand struggles, that the simple truth was arrived at, which is not by any means yet universally received,—the truth that the perception of external things through the organs of sense is a direct mental act—a phenomenon of consciousness not susceptible of being resolved into any thing else." *

Locke sometimes uses language which would indicate the doctrine of direct intuitive perception, but the theory which determined his thinking was the ideal theory.

"Whatsoever the mind perceives in itself, or is the immediate object of perception, thought, or understanding, that I call idea." † This implies that the object of perception is something in the mind. There is a confusion of the object of perception with the act of perception.

"Since extension, figure, number, and motion of bodies of an observable bigness, may be observed at a distance by the sight, it is evident some singly imperceptible bodies must come from them to the eyes, and thereby convey to the brain some motion, which produces these ideas which we have of them in us." ‡

This implies that the external objects are not directly perceived by the eye.

"It is evident that the mind knows not things

---

* Bailey. † Essay, Book I., chap. viii., sec. 8.
‡ Ibid., sec. 12.

immediately, but only by the intervention of the ideas it has of them. Our knowledge is therefore real, only so far as there is a conformity between our ideas and the reality of things. But what shall be here the criterion? How shall the mind, when it perceives nothing but its own ideas, know that they agree with things themselves? This, though it seems not to want difficulty, yet, I think, there be two sorts of ideas, that, we may be assured, agree with things." *

These extracts make it plain that Locke did not regard external objects as directly perceived by the mind. The direct object of perception was something intermediate. The mind "perceives nothing but its own ideas." He believed that there are external objects with which they agree—which they represent.

But if the mind perceives nothing but its own ideas, how can it know that there are any other things? How can it know that there are external things corresponding to these ideas? By concession, these external things are unperceived—unknown. The mind can cognize an agreement between two known things, but how can it cognize an agreement between a known object and an unknown one?

Locke admits that there is a difficulty, but thinks that "there be two sorts of ideas, that, we may be assured, agree with things."

* Essay, Book IV., chap. iv., sec. 3.

On Locke's theory of perception, it is plain, we can have no knowledge of any thing out of the mind. Idealism is the logical consequence of the theory. This remark is true with respect to every theory of mediate perception. If the object of the mind in perception be an idea, image, phantasm, and not external objects, then we have no knowledge of external objects. It may be affirmed that these ideas, images, phantasms, represent external objects. But of this, the advocates of the theory have no proof. They have therefore no ground for believing in the existence of an external world.

While Locke taught that the ideas, which are the objects of perception, represent external realities, Berkeley, with greater logical consistency, denied the existence of external realities.

"In common talk," says Berkeley, "the objects of our senses are not termed ideas, but things. Call them so still, provided you do not attribute to them any absolute existence, and I shall never quarrel with you for a word."

Again, he says: "It is an opinion strangely prevailing amongst men, that houses, mountains, rivers, and, in a word, all sensible objects, have an existence natural and real, distinct from their being perceived by the understanding. But with how great an assurance and acquiescence soever this principle may be entertained in this world, yet, whosoever shall find in his heart to call it in question, may, if I mis take not, perceive it to involve a manifest contradiction. For what are the prementioned objects, but the things we perceive by the sense; and what do we perceive besides our own ideas and sensations; and is it not plainly repugnant that any one of these, or any combination of them, should exist unperceived?"

Here the existence of any thing excepting our ideas and sensations is distinctly denied. The reasoning—if the term can properly be applied to a mere assumption and shifting of terms—is as follows:

Houses, mountains, and rivers, are the objects of our senses; but the only things we perceive by sense are our own ideas and sensations: hence houses, mountains, etc., have no existence except in the mind.

Houses, mountains, etc., are called ideas, and then all the qualities of ideas are ascribed to them. But to call a thing by the name of another thing, does not change the nature of the former to that of the latter. To call a horse a bird, does not change him into a bird.

It may be asked, Whence come our ideas of houses and mountains, if there are no such material objects to cause them? Berkeley would reply, that the Author of Nature "imprints them in the senses."

The following remarks from the pen of Bailey are deemed accurate: "Much as his [Berkeley's] arguments have been extolled, whoever closely examines them will find that he does not adduce a single one (arguments in a circle excepted) to prove his fundamental position; but, having assumed it without proof, he is thenceforward occupied partly in deducing conclusions from it, partly in explaining facts according to it, partly in contending with objections which nothing but his original assumption enables him to combat, partly in overcoming doctrines not necessarily held in connection with the absolute existence of an external world, and partly in attempting, by a retrograde process, to confirm the truth of the assumed proposition from its own consequences.

"That in doing this he has shown great logical adroitness and fertility of invention, much metaphysical knowledge and acumen, a wide range of thought, and a fluent and felicitous style, I most cheerfully admit."

CHAPTER VIII.

THEORIES OF PERCEPTION—REID—BROWN.

DR. THOMAS REID has the merit of overthrowing the theory of mediate perception—that is, the theory of perception through the agency of ideas intervening and bridging the space between matter and mind. Before his time that theory was very generally held. It is true that in many authors there may be found passages indicating correct views of perception; still the ideal theory influenced the general tone of philosophical thinking. The isolated passages referred to do not lessen the substantial merit of Reid in leading the way to more truthful views than had previously obtained general currency.

Reid saw the truth in regard to the perception of external objects, but did not see it with entire clearness. He saw that there was no intermediate object between the mind and the object perceived—that we have a direct, immediate, intuitive perception of external objects; but he did not discriminate accurately between sensation and perception. He sometimes used language adapted to make the impression that he regarded sensation as the instrument of perception. He taught that sensation always precedes perception. He says: "The impression made upon the organs, nerves, and brain, is followed by a sensation, and this sensation is followed by a perception of the object." Again: "The impression made upon the nerves and brain is performed behind the scenes, and the mind sees nothing of it. But every such impression, by the laws of the drama, is followed by a sensation which is the first scene exhibited to the mind, and this scene is quickly succeeded by another, which is the perception of the object."

Professor Dugald Stewart understood Reid to teach "that the mind is so formed that certain impressions produced upon our organs of sense by external objects, are followed by corresponding sensations, and that these sensations (which have no more resemblance to the qualities of matter than the words of language have to the things which they denote) are followed by a perception of the existence and qualities of the bodies by which the impressions are made."

"Every different perception," says Reid, "is conjoined with a sensation proper to it. The one is the sign, the other is the thing signified."

These expressions would seem to indicate that Reid regarded perception as an inference from sensation, and not a direct knowledge of the object. But he remarks: "We ask no argument for the existence of the object, but that we perceive it: perception commands our belief upon its own authority, and disdains to rest its authority upon any reasoning whatever." Exception may be taken to the use of the term belief in connection with perception, yet the passage shows that he regarded perception as a direct knowledge of the object—not a knowledge acquired by inference.

As was stated above, the defect in Reid's view of perception was owing to a want of accurate discrimination between sensation and perception. The distinction stated by Bailey is clear and satisfactory. Sensation is "an affection felt to be in some part of the body, whether attended or not by a discernment of any thing different from, or external to the sentient being." Perception is "discerning something different from, or external to, the percipient being, whether attended or not by a bodily sensation."

Sensation and perception are not always conjoined. We may have sensations without perceptions. Place a piece of ice near the body. A radiation of caloric from the body—a change in the condition of the body—will produce a sensation of cold or chilliness. This is in one sense a knowledge; that is to say, I know that I have in my body a sensation of chilliness; but it is not a perception, *i. e.*, a cognition of something external.

After long-continued bodily exertion, there is felt, in different parts of the body, a sensation of fatigue.

3*

This is not necessarily conjoined with the perception of any external object.

When one has gone without food for an unusual period, the condition of the stomach produces the sensation of hunger. This sensation is not in any way connected with the perception of any thing external. These sensations are feelings localized in the body. They are mental acts, states, or affections, clearly distinguishable from perceptions.

We may have perceptions without sensations. An object of sight is presented—a tree for example. The cognition is immediate. If we consult our consciousness, we shall find nothing but a direct cognition of the tree. The conditions of this cognition, the rays of light reflected from the object to the eye, the picture on the retina, the state of the optic nerve and the brain, are not within the sphere of consciousness. All that we are conscious of is an immediate perception of the tree. When the organ is in a healthy state, we are conscious of no feeling localized in the organ—no sensation. If the organ be diseased, a painful sensation may be felt in it, but the sensation has no connection with vision—that is, in no way contributes to it. It may be occasioned by nerves entirely distinct from the optic nerve.

Let the keys of a piano be struck: we hear a sound. Is it a sensation, that is, a feeling localized in the ear, or is it a cognition of sound? Plainly the latter. We cognize a sound. It is a mental act. We are conscious of the act, but are not ordinarily conscious of any local affection of the organ.

In case the ear is diseased, the vibrations of the atmosphere, one of the conditions of the mental act of hearing, may occasion a painful sensation. Even when the organ is in a healthy state, vibrations of great intensity, such as those occasioned by the explosion of a cannon near to one, will occasion a painful sensation.

Some writers have used the term sensation in connection with hearing, when they should have used the term emotion. They have spoken of the agreeable and disagreeable sensations of hearing, when they meant the agreeable or disagreeable emotions consequent upon the cognition of sounds. Some sounds are agreeable, and some disagreeable. An attendant or consequent emotion is one thing, a preceding sensation is another thing. The two things should not be confounded.

Perception by the sense of touch is attended by a sensation—a feeling localized in the organ. The sensation is separable in thought from the perception. Cognitions by the sense of taste and of smell are also attended with sensations. But a large portion of our perceptions are neither preceded nor attended by sensations. If the above remarks are correct, the reader will place a just estimate on Sir William Hamilton's law, the alleged discovery of which is claimed as one of his contributions to philosophy—" the grand law by which perception and sensation are governed by their reciprocal relation." This law, which Hamilton says "has been wholly overlooked by our psychologists," is thus stated: "Perception and sensation, though always coexistent, are always in the inverse ratio to each other."

Had Reid distinguished clearly between sensation and perception, there would have been no occasion for charging him with failing to teach the true doctrine of perception. That he held it substantially, no candid reader of his works can doubt.

Dr. Thomas Brown, whose "Lectures on the Philosophy of the Human Mind" furnish frequent examples of wonderful acuteness, taught, in regard to perception, that when an object is presented to our organs of sense, a certain mental state is occasioned, and this conscious state of mind is followed by an irresistible belief of the existence of the object causing said mental state.

. Brown discarded altogether the doctrine of ideas, that is, of a *tertium quid* between the object perceived and the perceiving mind, but he did not give a true account of the process of perception. He says, when an object is presented to the organs of sense, a mental state follows that presentation, and that state is followed by an irresistible belief of the existence of the object. But what is that mental state? When a table is placed before me, a mental state is produced. What is that mental state? It is a direct perception of the table. As soon as the light falls upon the table and is reflected to the eye, the mind sees the table. The conscious act or state of mind is a simple act or state, and cannot be analyzed into an act followed by an irresistible belief.

In consequence of his view of perception, Brown found great difficulty in determining the origin of our idea of externality. An object is presented to the senses, and produces a state of mind. All that we are conscious of is a state of mind—a subjective affection. We know that it must have a cause, but whether that cause be an external object or not, we cannot know, so long as we are destitute of the idea of externality. In attempting to account for the origin of our ideas of externality, he gives a striking specimen of ingenuity, but fails to remove the difficulty, which is of his own creation.

It is simply absurd to ask how we get the idea of externality in connection with our perception of external objects. When we cognize an external object, we cognize it as external. If we cognize it at all, we must cognize it as external to the mind and to the bodily organism. No one cognizing an object by one of the senses, ever cognized it as a mere modification of his own mind. The mind was made to cognize external objects. The idea of externality is necessarily involved in every cognition of matter.

Brown's doctrine of perception as logically leads to idealism, as does the doctrine of perception by means of ideas. If we are conscious of cognizing ideas only, then we have no means of knowing that there are external objects corresponding to those ideas. If, as Brown affirms, we are conscious only of a mental state, how can we know that the cause of that mental state has a material existence? Brown calls in the aid of an irresistible belief, but consciousness does not testify to the presence of said belief. It testifies to the direct cognition of the object.

CHAPTER IX.

THEORY OF SIR WILLIAM HAMILTON.

SIR WILLIAM HAMILTON claims to teach the doctrine of direct perception more emphatically than any of his predecessors. It is supposed by some that he corrected the errors of Reid and Brown, and gave an exposition of the philosophy of perception, at once convincing and exhaustive. A brief examination of his teachings may prove a useful exercise.

He teaches that the mind has a direct, immediate, intuitive perception of external objects. After a consideration of the various objections that have been made to the doctrine of direct perception, he remarks: "We have thus found, by an examination of the various grounds on which it has been attempted to establish the necessity of rejecting the testimony of consciousness to the intuitive perception of the external world, that the grounds are, one and all, incompetent."

He would extend the sphere of consciousness, so as to include the object perceived as well as the perceiving act. He insists on the propriety of saying,

"I am conscious of the inkstand," instead of saying, "I am conscious that I perceive the inkstand." "A slight consideration," he affirms, "is sufficient to reconcile us to the expression, as showing, if we hold the doctrine of immediate perception, the necessity of not limiting consciousness to our subjective states." Again he says: "The assertion that we can be conscious of the act of knowledge without being conscious of the object, is virtually suicidal."

The reader may be surprised to learn from Hamilton, who so strenuously contends for the authority of consciousness, that although "we are conscious of the inkstand," we do not see it. To be conscious of the inkstand must mean to be conscious that we see the inkstand. Yet, according to Hamilton, we do not see it. "We perceive, through no sense, aught external but what is in immediate relation and in immediate contact with its organ; and that is true, which Democritus of old asserted, that all our senses are only modifications of touch. Through the eye we perceive nothing but the rays of light in relation to, and in contact with, the retina; what we add to this perception must not be taken into account." "To say, for example, that we perceive by sight the sun or moon, is a false or an elliptical expression. We perceive nothing but certain modifications of light in immediate relation to our organ of vision; and so far from Dr. Reid being philosophically correct, when he says that, 'when ten men look at the sun or moon, they all see the same individual object,' the truth is that each of these persons sees a different object, because each person sees a different complement of rays in relation to his individual organ. In fact, if we look alternately with each, we have a different object in our right, and a different object in our left eye. It is not by perception, but by a process of reasoning, that we connect the objects of sense with existences beyond the sphere of immediate knowledge. It is enough that perception affords us the knowledge of the *non-ego* at the point of sense. To arrogate to it the power of immediately informing us of the existence of external things, which are only the cause of the objects which are immediately perceived, is either positively erroneous, or a confusion of language arising from an inadequate discrimination of the phenomena. Such assumptions tend only to throw discredit on the doctrine of intuitive perception; and such assumptions you will find scattered over the works both of Reid and Stewart. I would therefore establish as a fundamental position of the doctrine of immediate perception, the opinion of Democritus —that all our senses are only modifications of touch; in other words, that the external object of perception is always in contact with the organs of sense."

Do not the assumptions of Hamilton "tend to throw discredit on the doctrine of intuitive perception"? What are his assertions in regard to visible objects? We see only modifications of light, and different persons looking at the sun see different objects. Will it be said different rays of light enter different eyes? True, but does that fact prove that all do not see the same object? A cannon is fired: the undulations or portions of undulations that strike upon the tympanums of ten different persons are different; does that prevent their all hearing the same cannon?

The learned author confounds the condition of perception with the object of perception. The entrance of rays of light is a condition of perception. Every beholder of the sun is conscious of seeing it: he is not conscious of seeing certain modifications of light. In fact, he knows nothing about light, the retina, the optic nerve, till informed by the physiologist.

These assumptions of Hamilton are entirely inconsistent with the doctrine of direct, intuitive perception. If we see only rays of light, how do we know there is any thing but said rays? Hamilton stoutly contends that we must receive the attestations of consciousness as true. His whole doctrine of intuitive perception rests upon the truthfulness of consciousness. Now, we are as conscious that we see the inkstand when it is before us on the table, as we are that we feel it when we place our hand upon it. If Hamilton's assertion that we do not see the inkstand but only rays of light, be true, then consciousness is deceptive. If we are deceived as to seeing the inkstand, we may be deceived as to feeling the inkstand. All ground for certainty is gone.

Thus it appears that no man has more emphatically asserted the truthfulness of consciousness, and no man has more emphatically denied it.

He has made other assertions equally inconsistent with the doctrine of intuitive perception. When he insists on so direct a cognition that it is proper for us to say that we are conscious of the object, conscious of the inkstand, we have certainly a right to suppose that a real object is perceived. This he does not deny—in words at least. He affirms that "we perceive the material reality." "But what," he asks, "is meant by perceiving the material reality?" We give his answer; but shall be obliged to repeat his question, "What is meant?" in respect to several of his phrases. "In the first place," he says, in reply to the question, "it does not mean that we perceive the material reality absolutely and in itself; that is, out of relation to our organs or faculties." What is meant by "perceiving the material reality absolutely and in itself"? What is meant by the explanatory phrase "out of relation to our organs and faculties"?

Having told us, in his way, what is not meant by perceiving the material reality, he proceeds: "On the contrary, the total and real object of perception is the external object under relation to our sense and the faculty of cognition." What is meant by "under relation to our sense and the faculty of cognition"? He continues: "But though thus relative to us, the object is still no representation, no modification of the ego. It is the *non-ego*, modified and relative it may be, but still the non-ego. I formerly illustrated this to you by a supposition. Suppose that the total object in perception is 12; and suppose that the external reality contributes 6, the material sense 3, and the mind 3—this may enable you to form some rude conjecture of the nature of the object of perception." The material reality perceived is thus a compound of matter, sense, and mind! Consciousness says it is matter.

What modification does the non-ego receive from the mind? Suppose the non-ego to be a house; what modification does it receive at the hands of "the material sense," and "the mind," when perception takes place?

A house is before me: the light is reflected from the house to the eye, and an image of the house is formed on the retina. The optic nerve and the brain are in their normal state. A cognition takes place. The mind cognizes the house. All the facts mentioned as preceding the act of cognition are physiological conditions of the act. When these take place, the simple inexplicable act of cognition takes place. If cognizing the house is modifying it, it is so modified.

Hamilton tells us that the simple cognition is

made up of contributions from three sources, viz.: the house, the material sense, and the mind. The house contributes, say, one-half; the material structure of the eye one-third; and the mind one-third.

Consciousness gives us no information of this partnership. We are conscious of perceiving the house. If this consciousness is erroneous, and the object of perception is not the house, but a certain threefold combination, then consciousness is not trustworthy, and universal skepticism must be our portion.

Observe the impropriety of that mode of speaking, adopted by many writers, which represents knowledge as the joint contribution of mind and object. Mind and object are both necessary in order to knowledge, but it does not follow that knowledge is a compound of mind and object. What is the relation between mind and object? The mind knows, the object is known. That is the whole of the matter. If it be asked, How can the mind know? the conditions of the cognizing act may be stated, but the cognizing act cannot be described.

The following passage contains a doctrine of perception closely allied to, if not identical with, that held by Dr. Thomas Brown, and censured by Hamilton. "If it be asked," says Hamilton, "How do we know that this object (of perception) is not a mere mode of mind, illusively presented to us as a mode of matter? then, indeed, we must reply, that we do not in propriety know that what we are compelled to perceive-as not self—is not a perception of self; and that we can only on reflection believe such to be the case, in reliance upon the original necessity of so believing imposed on us by our nature."

After all, then, our knowledge of external objects as separate from the mind, is not a direct cognition, but an inevitable belief!

CHAPTER X.

RELATIVITY OF KNOWLEDGE.

MUCH has been said by late writers about the relativity of our knowledge, the tendency of which is to weaken the grounds of certainty of knowledge. We are told that "we know mind and matter not in themselves, but in their accidents and phenomena."

Hamilton affirms that "all human knowledge," consequently all human philosophy, "is only of the relative and phenomenal. In this proposition the term relative is opposed to the absolute; and, therefore, in saying that we know only the relative, I virtually assert that we know nothing absolute—nothing existing absolutely, in and for itself, and without relation to us and our faculties." Of course we cannot know that which has no relation to our faculties—that which is not an object of knowledge—that which is unknowable. The distinction, then, between the relative and the absolute, is simply the distinction between that which can be known and that which cannot be known. It is granted that our knowledge is limited. We know but in part. Beyond and connected with all that is known, there is much that is unknown. If the terms relative and absolute were intended to express this distinction, they were not happily chosen; for when we are told our knowledge is only relative and phenomenal, there is a tendency to regard it as unsubstantial. If the terms were not intended to express this distinction, what were they intended to express? What is meant by "existing absolutely and of itself, without relation to us and our faculties"? How is it known that there are objects existing out of relation to our faculties? If we are authorized to affirm that there are such objects, that affirmation is knowledge. How came the existence of these unknown and unknowable objects to be known? If an object is without relation to our faculties, it cannot be cognized by our faculties, and of course its existence cannot be affirmed.

Hamilton proceeds to illustrate the assertions above quoted: "I shall illustrate this by its application. Our knowledge is either of matter or of mind. Now, what is matter? What do we know of matter? Matter, or body, is to us the name either of something known or of something unknown. In so far as matter is the name of something known, it means that which appears to us under the forms of extension, solidity, divisibility, figure, motion, roughness, smoothness, color, heat, cold, etc.; in short, it is a common name for certain series, aggregate, or complement of appearances or phenomena manifested in coexistence. But as the phenomena appear only in conjunction, we are compelled, by the constitution of our nature, to think them conjoined in and by something; and as they are phenomena, we cannot think them the phenomena of nothing, but must regard them as the properties or qualities of something that is extended, solid, figured, etc. But this something, absolutely and in itself—*i. e.*, considered apart from its phenomena—is to us as zero. It is only in its qualities, only in its effects, in its relative or phenomenal existence, that it is cognizable or conceivable. It is only by a law of thought that compels us to think of something absolute and unknown as the basis or condition of the relative and known, that something obtains a kind of incomprehensible reality to us. Now, that which manifests its qualities—in other words, that in which the appearing causes inhere, that to which they belong—is called, then, *subject*, or *substance*, or *substratum*. To this subject of the phenomena of extension, solidity, etc., the term *matter*, or *material substance*, is commonly given; and therefore, as contradistinguished from these qualities, it is the name of something unknown and inconceivable."

The same doctrine in regard to our knowledge of matter was taught by Professor Dugald Stewart. "It is not matter or body which I perceive by my senses, but only extension, color, figure, and certain other qualities which the constitution of my nature leads me to refer to something which is extended, figured, colored."

In opposition to these high authorities, it may be safely affirmed that it is not true that we perceive extension, figure, color, etc., and infer the existence of something in which they inhere. We intuitively cognize matter or body as extended, figured, colored, etc. If we do not cognize matter—body—directly, we cognize nothing directly. If we do not know what matter is, we do not know what any thing is. Extension, and color, and other facts in relation to matter, when considered apart from body, are mere abstractions; and abstractions are not known entities inhering in an unknown something. We can consider extension, solidity, color, etc., abstractly, but that is not cognizing them as entities belonging to an unknown substratum. We cognize body as extended, divisible, colored, etc. If the use of abstract terms had been avoided in relation to body, the doctrine of a *substratum*, and of a relative knowledge of matter, would not have been known. It is the offspring of scholastic abstraction.

The position I have taken is supported by one of the most sober and accurate thinkers of the day. "I can see," says McCosh, "no evidence whatever for the existence of any such thing as a *substratum*, lying in or beyond, or standing under all that comes under our immediate knowledge. There is no topic on which there has been a greater amount of unintelligible language employed than on this. We know, it is said, only qualities; but we are constrained by reason, or by common sense, to believe in a something in which they inhere. Or, qualities, it is said, fall under sense, while substance is known by reason. Others, proceeding on these admissions, maintain that, qualities alone being known, we may doubt whether there is such a thing as substance, and may certainly affirm that we can never know it. Now, in opposition to all this style of thinking and of writing, which has prevailed to so great an extent since the days of Locke, I maintain that we never know qualities without also knowing substance. Qualities, as qualities, distinct from substances, are as much unknown to us as substance distinct from qualities."

Again: "It is very common to say that substance is a thing behind the qualities, or underneath them, acting as a substratum, basis, ground, or support. All such language is in its very nature metaphorical; the analogy is of the most distant kind, and may have a misleading character. The substance is the very thing itself considered in a certain aspect, and the qualities are its action or manifestation. Again, it is frequently said that qualities are known, whereas substance cannot be known, or, if known, known only by some deeper or more transcendental principle of the mind. Now, I hold that we never know quality except as the quality of a substance, and that we know both equally in one undivided act. This is a somewhat less mystical and mysterious account than that commonly given by metaphysicians, but is, as it appears to me, in strict accordance with the revelations of consciousness."

We are told by some writers, that the essence of matter and mind is unknown. The author above quoted says of essence: "It is a very mystical word, and a whole aggregate of foolish speculations has clustered around it." "We are not warranted to maintain that there must be something lying further in than the qualities we know, and that this something is entitled to be regarded as the essence of the object. We have no ground whatever for believing that there must be, or that there is, something more internal or central than the substance and quality which we know. True, there are probably occult qualities even in those objects with which we are most intimately acquainted; but we are not therefore warranted to conclude, that what is concealed must differ in nature or in kind from what is revealed, or that it is in any way more necessary to the existence or the continuance of the object. I have a shrewd suspicion that there is a vast amount of unmeaning talk in the language which is employed on this special subject by metaphysicians, who would see something which the vulgar cannot discern, whereas they should be contented with pointing to what all men perceive. It is quite conceivable, and perfectly probable, that though we should know all about any given terrestrial or material object, we should, after all, not fall in with any thing more mysterious or deep than those wonders which come every day under our notice in the world without, and the world within us."

The following are the views of this author in regard to existence in itself: "I cannot give my adhesion to the opinion of those who speak so strongly of man being incapacitated to know Being. I have already intimated my dissent from that Kantian doctrine, that we do not know things, but appearances; and even from the theory of those Scottish metaphysicians who affirm that we do not know things, but qualities. What we know, is the thing manifesting itself to us—is the thing exercising particular qualities. But then it is confidently asserted that we do not know the 'thing in itself.' The language, I rather think, is unmeaning; but if it has a meaning, it is incorrect. I do not believe that there is any such thing in existence as Being in itself, or that man can even so much as imagine it; and if this be so, it is clear that we cannot know it, and desirable that we should not suppose that we know it. Of this I am sure, that those Neo-Platonists who professed to be able to rise to the discovery of Being in itself (which could only be the abstract idea of Being), and to be employed in gazing on it, had miserably bare and most unprofitable matter of meditation whether for intellectual, or moral, or religious ends. But if any mean to deny that we can know Being as it is, I maintain in opposition to them, and I appeal to consciousness to confirm me, when I say, that we immediately know Being in every act of cognition. But then we are told that we cannot know the mystery of Being. I am under a strong impression that speculators have attached a much greater amount of mystery to this simple subject than really belongs to it. Of this I am sure, that much of the obscurity which has collected around it has sprung from the confused discussions of metaphysicians, who have labored to explain what needs no explanation to our intelligence, or to get a basis on which to build what stands securely on its own foundation. I do indeed most fully admit, that there may be much about Being which we do not know; much about Being generally, much about every individual Being, unknown to us, and unknowable to us in this world. Still, I do affirm that we know so much of Being, and that any further knowledge conveyed to us would not set aside our present knowledge, but would simply enlarge it." *

The following remarks in regard to the phrase, "knowing things in themselves," are by Bailey:

"It is worth while to advert more particularly to the proposition often reiterated by Kant, that we cannot know things in themselves—a proposition extensively accepted by philosophers.

* McCosh's "Intuitions of the Mind," p. 163.

"This is, in my view, a perfectly unmeaning assertion. We cannot form the slightest conception of knowing external things, except as we do know them, *i. e.*, through the organs of sense. Do you demur at this? Then be so good as to tell me the precise signification of knowing things in themselves; give me a specimen of that sort of knowledge which we have not; and point out how you have gained so envious a piece of transcendental information.

"No one, manifestly, is entitled to deny that our knowledge is of things in themselves, unless he not only possesses the sort of knowledge which he denies to others, and has found, in comparison, that we—the rest of the human race—have only a knowledge of things as they are not in themselves, but actually produces it for our examination. Till that is done, assertions about knowing things in themselves must be regarded as utterly without meaning."

CHAPTER XI.

REMARKS ON THE NATURE OF PERCEPTION.

IT has not been my design to give an historical account of the various theories of perception. I have noticed some errors, for the purpose of enabling the student to get a clearer view of the truth. On this, as on many other subjects, the simple truth has been overlooked, and almost every conceivable form of error has been adopted, and exploded. The true doctrine of perception is very simple, and has always been held by all except philosophers. It is sometimes asked, Can the existence of an external world be proved? The reply is, It is an object of direct cognition, and hence is not susceptible of proof or disproof. "For, let us pause a moment, and reflect what constitutes proof—what proof is. It is neither more nor less than some fact which causes us, or which is adduced for the purpose of causing us, to discern or to believe some other fact.

" Now, a fact must be either external or internal, material or mental, relating to the world without or the world within. But an external fact cannot be adduced in proof that there are such things as external objects; for that would be alleging as evidence the very truth to be proved. Nor can it be adduced in disproof; for that would be affirming the positive existence of a thing in order to disprove its existence.

"But if an external fact cannot, in this case, be brought forward in proof or disproof, it is equally plain that a purely mental or internal fact cannot be adduced for either purpose.

"The only mental or internal fact which can be mentioned as at all relating to the subject, is, that we perceive external objects: but this cannot, of course, be alleged in proof of itself, or of its own truth; nor can it be brought, without egregious absurdity, in disproof of itself.

"That there are external objects perceived by us, is, therefore, a primary fact, which admits neither of being proved nor disproved; and it is amazing that philosophers of great depth and power have attempted to do either." *

The following remarks by the author above quoted are worthy of attention:

"When we perceive an object, we have not any consciousness of the conditions of the nerves and brain concerned in the resulting act of perception, nor of the motions of any inorganic medium between the object and our organ: we are conscious of per-

* Bailey

ceiving the external object, and nothing else. In seeing, we are not conscious of the retina, nor of the rays of light impinging upon it, nor of the picture there delineated. In hearing, we are not conscious of the drum of the ear, nor of the pulses of the air by which it is struck, nor, in either case, of any communication between those parts and the brain.

"As we are unconscious of the physical process, so what we are conscious of perceiving is not at all affected by our being able or unable to trace that process of which perception is the result. In other words, our perception of external objects is not alterable by any insight or want of insight into its physical causes. What is designated by the words 'seeing an object,' is the same mental state in the child, the savage, the philosopher, and as a simple modification of consciousness neither wants nor admits of any analysis or explanation. Although the physical events leading to it may be minutely investigated, it cannot itself be resolved into any mental state or states. You may trace the course of light from the object to the organ, you may follow its refractions by the lens of the eye, you may detect the picture on the retina, you may explore the connection of the optic nerve with the brain; but you do not, by all these discoveries, valuable as they are, alter in the slightest degree the resulting state of consciousness denominated seeing the object. Although they are facts in the physical process absolutely necessary to the result, a knowledge of them does not in the least modify the consequent perception. Hence it follows that no extent of investigation, no discovery in science, can ever change the character of our acquaintance with external objects. If we could push our insight of nature to the utmost imaginable extreme, if we could ascertain the shape and pursue the movements of every particle of matter in the world around us, we should still have only the same *kind* of knowledge, although highly exalted in degree, which we have now; we should still be acquainted with the material universe only through our sensitive organs. The telescope and the microscope, while they extend the reach of our senses, do not in the slightest degree alter the nature of our perceptions. And further, all the various steps in the physical process through which we become cognizant of any external object are external objects themselves, and are perceived in the same way as the rest."

CHAPTER XII.

COGNITION OF MENTAL OPERATIONS—PERSONALITY—
IDENTITY—CEASELESS ACTIVITY—CONSCIOUSNESS.

We have seen that the mind can cognize the existence and qualities of material objects. But material objects are not the sole objects of knowledge. We do not acquire all our knowledge through the agency of the senses.

The mind can cognize its own existence and operations. If it be asked, How can the mind be at the same time both subject and object of knowledge? we can only reply, such is the fact. Our knowledge of a fact is not destroyed by our ignorance of the manner in which the fact takes place.

We have a direct cognition of our mental operations. We do not, it is true, see them by the eye, or hear them by the ear, but we have a direct cognition of them.

We have also a direct cognition of our existence. Whenever the mind cognizes the existence of an object, it cognizes its own existence. In the consciousness of cognizing the object is involved the consciousness of cognizing its own existence. In every mental act there is a direct cognition of the existence of the mind. Some writers affirm that we are conscious only of our mental acts or states, and that the existence of the mind is an inference—a necessary inference, indeed, but still an inference—from those mental acts or states. Thus I am conscious of an act, therefore there must be an agent.

Professor Stewart, one of the few men who have not been overrated by their admirers, says: "We are not immediately conscious of its (the mind's) existence, but we are conscious of sensation, thought, and volition, operations which imply the existence of something which feels, thinks, and wills."

No doubt the existence of thought implies a thinker, just as the existence of a watch implies a maker. In the latter case, the inference is separable in thought from the fact. But not so in regard to the thinker. The cognition of the existence of the thinker is contemporaneous with and inseparable from the conscious thought. The consciousness of the existence of the mind operating is an integral part of the conscious act. The perceiving agent and the thing perceived are embraced in the same act of consciousness.

Professor Mansel teaches the doctrine of a direct cognition. "Is it not," he says, "a flat contradiction to maintain that I am not immediately conscious of myself, but only of my sensations or volitions? Who then is this *I* that is conscious, and how can *I* be conscious of such states as MINE? In this case it would surely be far more accurate to say, not that I am conscious of my sensations, but that the sensation is conscious of itself; but thus worded, the glaring absurdity of the theory would carry with it its own refutation." " The one *presented substance*, the source from which our data for thinking on the subject are originally drawn, is *myself*. Whatever may be the variety of the phenomena of consciousness, sensations by this or that organ, volitions, thoughts, imaginations, of all we are immediately conscious as affections of one and the same self. It is not by any afterthought of reflection that I combine together sight, hearing, thought, and volition, into a factitious unity or compounded whole; in each case I am immediately conscious of myself seeing and hearing, willing and thinking. This self-personality, like all other simple apprehensions, is indefinable, but it is so because it is superior to definition. It can be analyzed into no simple element, for it is itself the simplest of all; it can be made no clearer by description or comparison, for it is revealed to us in all the clearness of an original intuition, of which description and comparison can furnish only faint and partial resemblances."

We cognize the mind as existing as a person, not as a thing. To be conscious of our existence, is to be conscious of our existence as persons. Some would appear to find difficulty in determining in what personality consists, just as they find difficulty in determining in what truth consists and in what existence consists. To inquire in what our personality consists, is to inquire in what we consist. An inanimate thing has certain qualities, that is, there are certain things or facts true concerning it. The same is true of a brute and of a person. We can inquire what things are true of each, and can thus learn what things are peculiar to each. This covers the whole ground of inquiry open to us. The main fact characteristic of a person as distinguished from a brute is, that a person has the power of cognizing duty, and of acting freely in relation to it.

To cognize the mind as a person, is to cognize it as one—as having unity. We are conscious of numerous operations, but we are conscious of them as the operations of one operator. The question, What is one? in what does unity consist? cannot be answered. The mind is capable of knowing many things which it cannot describe or explain. Every simple elementary idea, every intuition, belongs to this class. It is scarcely necessary to observe that none of these things need to be described or explained.

It is said by some, that, while we cognize the existence and operations of the mind, we do not cognize its nature. The nature of an object is not something different from the object, as many seem to imagine. Suppose an object possesses four properties; that is, there are four things cognizable, true, concerning it. When we have cognized those four things, is there still something different from them remaining unknown, viz., its nature? The questions, What is a thing, and what is its nature? are identical. A recognition of this truth would have saved many discussions.

When the question is asked respecting a thing, What is it? the answer states facts concerning it. To tell what a thing is fully, is to state all facts belonging to it; that is, every thing that is true concerning it—all its properties or qualities. If it be a compound object, its constituent elements as well as its qualities are stated. If it be a simple object, its qualities are stated. If, when the question, What is a thing? has thus been answered, the question is still asked, What is its nature? the answer will consist of a statement of its most prominent characteristics or qualities, but said characteristics or qualities will be found among the facts stated in answer to the question, What is it?

The mind continues to be the same mind amid all changes of its operations and conditions, and all changes of the body. The conscious operations of to-day may differ widely from those of yesterday; but I am as certain that I am the same person that I was yesterday, as I am that I exist to-day.

The doctrine of personal identity requires no proof. It is intuitively perceived. Why, then, it may be asked, have there been discussions and disputes about it? Disputes imply difficulties.

Difficulties always arise when men try to prove self-evident truths, or to answer questions which are unanswerable. Locke attempted to answer the question, "In what does our identity consist?" and, of course, fell into confusion of thought. Unable to answer the question, he unwittingly answered in its stead, ".On what is our cognition of identity conditioned?"

The cognition of identity is conditioned on an act of remembrance. If we could not remember any past act, we could have no idea of personal identity. Our knowledge would be confined to our present existence and present acts. When we remember a mental act, we remember it as our act. The idea of identity is involved in every act of remembrance. Identity does not depend upon memory, but memory is the necessary condition of cognizing it. Our cognition of personal identity is thus an intuition conditioned on an act of remembrance.

Is the mind always active? Are its operations ceaseless? We know from experience that it is always active during our waking hours. Its action is sometimes sluggish and sometimes rapid, but it always acts—always exists in some active state. Is it always active during sleep? Sleep seems to be a bodily affection solely. It consists in the temporary inability of the organs of sense to perform their functions. We know that the mind is active up to the time when sleep takes place. We know that we often dream; that is, we remember operations that took place when we were asleep. We know that we dream more when our sleep is broken than when it is sound. We know that the mind is active as soon as sleep is removed. We sometimes have dreams, that is, mental operations take place during sleep, which we do not remember; for we are observed to speak in sleep, and do not remember it when we awake. The probability is that the mind in its normal state is always active.

Is the mind always conscious of its operations? or can it perform unconscious processes? Those who affirm that the mind can perform acts of which it is unconscious, state, as example, the case of the striking of a clock when one is reading. He does not hear it, he says. You must have heard it, says his friend, for it has just struck. I was not conscious of it. Was it a case of unconscious hearing? or did he hear it, but, in consequence of paying no attention to it, forget it?

Often a man has been told that he has performed a certain act. He affirms, in all honesty, that he has not performed it. Some time afterwards he remembers the act. But for that accidental remembrance, the act might be quoted as an example of unconscious mental operation.

A person is reading aloud. His attention wanders. He turns the leaf, but is perfectly ignorant of the ideas expressed on the pages read. His mind has been occupied by some other topic. He must have cognized the letters and words, and performed acts of will causing utterance. Were those acts unconsciously performed, or were they consciously performed, but immediately forgotten in consequence of the lack of attention? Some degree of attention, we know, is necessary, in order that we may remember.

A skilful musician performs a piece of music on the piano. Is there a volition connected with every movement of the fingers? When he first began to play, he was conscious of a distinct volition in connection with every movement. When a high degree of skill has been attained, he is not conscious of any such volition. He is conscious only of a general purpose to perform the piece. Do the volitions take place unconsciously? Reid says, the action of the fingers in this case is mechanical—an illustration of what he calls a mechanical habit. An objection to Reid's view is found in the fact, that if a false note is struck, it is instantly perceived and corrected. This would indicate attention, though the person may not be conscious of bestowing it.

Stewart says there is conscious volition antecedent to each movement. He says: "I cannot help thinking it more philosophical to suppose that those actions which are originally voluntary always continue so, although in the case of operations which have become habitual in consequence of long practice, we may not be able to recollect every different volition. Thus, in the case of a performer on the harpsichord, I apprehend that there is an act of the will preceding every motion of the fingers, although he may not be able to recollect these volitions afterwards, and although he may, during the time of his performance, be employed in carrying on a separate train of thought. For it must be remarked, that the most rapid performer can, when he pleases, play so slowly as to be able to attend to and to recollect every separate act of his will in the various movements of his fingers, and he can gradually accelerate the rate of his execution till he is unable to recollect these acts. Now, in this instance, one of two suppositions must be made. The one is, that the operations in the two cases are carried on in precisely the same manner, and differ only in the degree of rapidity; and the other, that when this rapidity exceeds a certain rate, the operation is taken entirely out of our hands, and is carried on by some unknown power, of the nature of which we are as ignorant as we are of the cause of the circulation of the blood, or of the motion of the intestines. The last supposition seems to me to be somewhat similar to that of a man who should maintain, that although a body projected with a moderate velocity is seen to pass through all the intermediate spaces in moving from one place to another, yet we are not entitled to conclude that this happens when the body moves so quickly as to become invisible to the eye.

"The former supposition is supported by the analogy of many other facts in our constitution. An expert accountant, for example, can sum up, almost at a single glance of his eye, a long column of figures. He can tell the sum with unerring certainty, while, at the same time, he is unable to recollect any one of the figures of which that sum is composed; and yet nobody doubts that each one of these figures has passed through his mind, or supposes that when the rapidity of the process becomes so great that he is unable to recollect the various steps, he obtains the result by a sort of inspiration."

Sir William Hamilton advocates the doctrine of unconscious mental agency. He asks: "Are there, in ordinary, mental modifications, *i. e.*, mental activities and passivities, of which we are unconscious, but which manifest their existence by effects of which we are conscious?"

That there are mental modifications beyond the sphere of consciousness, is doubtless true; our habits and dispositions are examples of such modifications; but are there such modifications as may properly be termed activities beyond the sphere of consciousness? Are there any unconscious mental activities?

"Let us take our first example," says Hamilton, "from perception—the perception of external objects—and in that faculty let us commence with the sense of sight. Now, you either already know, or can at once be informed, what it is that has obtained the name of the *Minimum Visibile*. You are, of course, aware in general, that vision is the result of the rays of light reflected from the surface of objects to the eye; a greater number of rays is reflected from a larger surface: if the superficial extent of an object, and, consequently, the number of rays which it reflects, be diminished beyond a certain limit, the object becomes invisible; and the minimum visibile is the smallest expanse which can be seen—which can consciously affect us—which we can be conscious of seeing. This being understood, it is plain that if we divide the minimum visibile into two parts, neither half can, by itself, be an object of vision, or visual consciousness. They are, severally and apart, to consciousness as zero. But it is evident that each half must, by itself, have produced in us a certain modification, real, though unperceived; for as the perceived whole is nothing but the union of the unperceived halves, so the perception—the perceived affection itself of which we are conscious—is only the sum of two modifications, each of which severally eludes our consciousness."

The above does not prove that we can perform unconscious acts. There is, on the part of the author, a failure to distinguish between a material or physiological condition of perception and the mental act of perception. The conscious perception of the minimum visibile is not made up of two unconscious perceptions. We may admit that each half of the expanse has produced a certain modification of the organism of sense; but a modification of the organism of sense is one thing, and the modification of a mental act is another. The two must not be confounded. Assume that the modification is a mental act, and you have an example of an unconscious mental act; but the modification is not a mental act, but the condition of a mental act.

The whole expanse perceived is the union of the two halves; but it does not follow that the perception of the whole, considered as a mental act, is made up of two half perceptions considered as mental acts. His remarks are tantamount to this. The minimum visibile produces a perception; therefore half of it must produce half a perception: but we are not conscious of the half perception; therefore we have unconscious perceptions.

Suppose a pair of scales, with an ounce weight in one of the scales. Put another ounce weight in the other scale, and it will bring that side down to a level with the other. No one would say that half an ounce will bring it down halfway. An ounce is the smallest weight that will bring down the scale, and so the minimum visibile is the smallest expanse that will produce perception. Each half of the minimum visibile produces a modification of the organ of sense, on which the mental act is conditioned.

Again he says: "When we look at a distant forest, we perceive a certain expanse of green. Of this, as an affection of our organism, we are clearly and distinctly conscious. Now, the expanse of which we are conscious is evidently made up of parts of which we are not conscious. No leaf, perhaps no tree, may be separately visible. But the greenness of the forest is made up of the greenness of the leaves; that is, the total impression of which we are conscious is made up of an infinitude of small impressions of which we are not conscious."

Here the impressions upon the organs of sense, which are among the conditions of perception, are confounded with the mental act of perception. We are conscious of perceiving the outline and color of the forest. Whatever impressions were made upon the organs of sense, whatever rays of light were reflected from whatever number of leaves, are the conditions of perception, and not the mental act of perception. Those conditions are not within the sphere of consciousness; they are modifications of the material organs. One is not authorized to say, "Modifications of the material organs may take place without our being conscious of them; therefore mental acts may take place without our being conscious of them."

"Take another example," says Hamilton, "from the sense of hearing. In this sense there is, in like manner, a *Minimum Audibile;* that is, a sound the least that can come into perception and consciousness. But this minimum audibile is made up of parts which severally affect the sense, but of which affections, separately, we are not conscious, though of their joint result we are. We must, therefore, here likewise admit the reality of modifications beyond the sphere of consciousness. Take a special example. When we hear the distant murmur of the sea, what are the constituents of the total perception of which we are conscious ? This murmur is a sum made up of parts, and the sum would be as zero if the parts did not count as something. The noise of the sea is a complement of the noise of its several waves; and if the noise of each wave made no impression on our sense, the noise of the sea, as the result of these impressions, could not be realized. But the noise of each several wave, at the distance we suppose, is inaudible; we must, however, admit that they produce a certain modification, beyond consciousness, on the recipient subject; for this is necessarily involved in the reality of their result."

One wave is inaudible, but a hundred waves are audible. Therefore the audible is made up of one hundred inaudibles ; the conscious mental act is made up of one hundred unconscious mental modifications. If by "modifications on the recipient subject" he does not mean mental modifications, then the point for which he is contending, viz., unconscious mental operations, is not reached. He confounds here, as above, impressions on the organism of sense—conditions of perception—with the act of perception.

The vibrations caused by one wave fail to affect the ear so as to produce a cognition of sound; the vibration of one hundred waves do so affect the ear as to produce a cognition of sound. This is a fair statement of the facts of the case. It furnishes no proof of unconscious mental agency.

The fact that the mind may possess latent knowledge, does not prove that it can perform unconscious mental acts. The condition of the mind, as distinguished from acts of the mind, is, of course, beyond the sphere of consciousness. A habit is a condition of the mind which is manifested by effects—conscious acts. A condition of mind may be termed a modification of mind, but it cannot properly be termed a mental agency. Hamilton does not use the term "unconscious mental operation;" but if he is not arguing in behalf of the proposition that such operations may take place, he is arguing for that which no one ever disputed.

The case of the somnambulist does not furnish an example of unconscious mental action. He gives abundant proof, when in that state, that he is conscious of his actions—that he knows what he is about. When he is awake, he has no remembrance of what took place in his sleep. To forget and to be unconscious, are not identical.

Cases of disordered mental action seem to furnish examples of unconscious mental action. Admitting that unconscious mental action does take place in cases of disease, the question still remains, Can the mind, when it is in its normal state, perform operations of which it is unconscious?

CHAPTER XIII.

COGNITION OF SPACE.

THERE is a difference between knowing what a thing is, and telling what it is. Our inability to define or describe a thing does not authorize us to deny its existence. Every one knows there is such a thing as truth, *i. e.*, true propositions; but no one can tell what truth is. If the question be asked, In what does truth consist? no answer can be given. There is no such thing as truth apart from true propositions; as there is no such thing as life apart from living things. When it is said we cannot cognize being in itself, if by being in itself is meant existence apart from things existing, the assertion is true, for there is no such thing. That which is not, we cannot cognize.

Of a provable proposition the question may be asked, In what does its truth consist—*i. e.*, on what proof does it rest? But if the question be asked with respect to a self-evident proposition, such as that the whole is greater than its part, no answer can be given. You may say it consists in being true, but that is only an awkward re-affirmance.

We cannot tell what an act of perception is. Do you say it is a mental act? What kind of a mental act? An act of perceiving. What kind of mental act is an act of perceiving? To this question we can give no answer. If asked in what it consists, we can only answer, It consists in perceiving. We are not, then, to call in question the reality of a thing, merely because we are not able to tell what it is, or in what it consists.

We have seen that our cognition of identity is not a remembrance, but an intuition conditioned upon a remembrance. An intuitive cognition may thus be conditioned on a preceding act of mind. Such a cognition is distinguishable from an inference properly so called.

We can cognize space. The cognition of space is intuitive, though it is conditioned on the cognition of body. If we had no knowledge of body, it does not appear that we should have any knowledge of space.

When we cognize an object as existing, we cognize it as existing in space. We are as conscious that we cognize it in space, as we are that we cognize it at all. The two cognitions are inseparable. Space, then, exists independently of the mind which cognizes it. The tree which we cognize as existing in space, exists when it is not perceived. We have the same ground for asserting that space exists when it is not perceived, as we have for asserting that the tree exists when it is not perceived. Consciousness does not affirm that the mind creates space: it affirms that the mind cognizes it. It is not, then, a creation of the mind, a subjective state, as is held by Kant, Hamilton, Whewell, and others.

"According to Kant," says McCosh, "space and time are forms given by the mind to the phenomena which are presented through the senses, and are not to be considered as having any thing more than a subjective existence. It is one of the most fatal heresies—that is, dogmas opposed to the revelations of consciousness—ever introduced into philosophy, and it lies at the basis of all the aberrations in the school of speculation which followed. For those who were taught that the mind could create space and time, soon learned to suppose that the mind could also create the objects and events cognized as existing in space and time, till the whole external universe became ideal, and all reality was supposed to lie in a series of connected mental forms."

McCosh frankly admits that there are difficulties connected with space as an objective existence. "But," he remarks, "it is of all courses the most foolish and suicidal to urge the difficulties connected with space and time as a reason for setting aside our intuitive convictions respecting them, say in regard to their reality. Doubtless we are landed in some perplexities by allowing that they are real, but we are landed in more hopeless difficulties and in far more serious consequences when we deny their reality; and there is this important difference in the cases, that in the one the difficulties arise from the nature of the subject, whereas in the other they are created by our own unwarranted affirmations and speculations."

Professor D. Stewart says: "We have an irresistible conviction that space is necessarily existent, and that its annihilation is impossible. To call this proposition in question, is to open the door to universal skepticism."

If we are asked, What is space? in what does it consist? we answer, we cannot tell. Our inability to state in what space consists, does not prove that it does not exist. Our inability to state in what the Divine Existence consists, does not prove that there is no Divine Existence.

Space is not a material existence. It is extended, but it has not material extension. When we cognize it, we do not cognize it as possessing any of the qualities of matter. It has not gravity, solidity, or visible and tangible form. It has no one of the qualities of matter.

Space is not a spiritual existence; it is not an existence that thinks, feels, and wills. We have no proof that it thinks, feels, and wills; no reason to suppose that it does.

Will it be asked, If it be not a material nor spiritual existence, what kind of existence is it? We reply,

It is space. All existences do not of necessity come under the head of material and spiritual existences. It does not follow that if space be neither material nor spiritual, there is no such thing. We know that it is; we cognize its existence.

Space is not an attribute of God, as was assumed by Dr. Samuel Clark. God is a spirit. His attributes are the attributes of a spiritual being. Space, we have seen, is not a spiritual existence, and for the same reason we may affirm that it is not the attribute of a spiritual being.

Space is limitless. When the mind makes it the object of attention, it sees that it can have no limit. If it be asked how the mind can see so far, I reply: We are not called upon to tell how a thing is done, in order to know that it is done. We cognize the fact that all truth is consistent; that two propositions, one directly in conflict with the other, cannot be true. Our conviction of the proposition is not an inference .from a number of experiences. The first time we found an assertion in conflict with a known truth, we knew it was false. We are just as sure that truth is consistent with itself in Jupiter as on the earth, though our minds have never made an excursion to that planet.

If the mind can cognize the fact that truth is everywhere consistent with itself throughout the universe, may it not cognize the fact that space is limitless?

It is common to say that space is limitless, because we cannot conceive of its being limited. A mode of expression more strictly accordant with our consciousness is, that the mind sees that space can have no limits.

Conceivability or non-conceivability is not a test of truth. The phrase, "I cannot conceive of it," has two meanings which must not be confounded. Two hills cannot exist without an intervening valley. Why not? I cannot conceive of such a thing, is the reply. The phrase thus used expresses our cognition of the impossibility of the thing. The mind sees that it cannot be.

A person ignorant of the existence of a magnetic telegraph is assured, on evidence that he cannot doubt, that a message was sent to California and an answer returned the same day. He says, I cannot conceive of such a thing! The phrase expresses his ignorance of the manner in which the communication took place.

Space always has existed, and always will exist. This is a bold affirmation; but it is one which the mind is abundantly competent to make. Suppose that all material objects were annihilated: we know that space would remain. Go back in thought to the era of creation: space existed then. The mind sees that it always must have existed, as clearly as it sees that the whole is greater than its part.

Space is not divisible; that is, it is not divisibl
5*

in the sense in which matter is divisible. Matter is divided when the parts are separated so that space intervenes. Space cannot be thus divided. We cannot separate space from space.

Space is not made up of parts, yet it may be said to have parts or portions. A portion larger or smaller may be occupied by created objects; yet space is not made up of portions as the earth is made up of portions.

Points in space may be taken, and these points may sustain certain relations to each other. The science of geometry has for its subject-matter the relations of space. We can take a finite portion of space, and cognize its relations; yet the infinite is not made up of multiplications of the finite.

CHAPTER XIV.

COGNITION OF TIME.

WHEN we remember an event, we remember it as past. We thus have a cognition of time. The cognition is involved in every act of remembrance. We know that all events take place in time.

What is time? It is sometimes said that it is a portion of duration measured by the revolution of the heavenly bodies. But it may be asked, What is duration? We cannot give a definition or description of duration. Yet we know that duration is. Like space, it is neither a material nor a spiritual existence. It is not a creation of the mind or form of our cognitions, as is asserted by Kant and others—whatever that phrase may mean.

Duration had no beginning, and will have no end. The ground of this assertion is, that the mind sees that there never could have been a time when duration was not. We turn to the past, and see that there could not have been a starting point to duration. We turn to the future, and see that it must continue to be. Time, duration as measured by the sun, may be no longer; but duration must go on forever.

It is thought by some, that what we have described as acts of cognition, are really acts of imagination. We go back or forward, it is said, in imagination, and find no beginning or end of duration; but our imaginations are not cognitions. I affirm that we cognize the fact that duration never began and never will have an end. It is a question to be decided by an appeal to consciousness. Do we not know that duration will never be ended? Are we not as certain of it as we are that the sun exists? This is not cognizing a fact at an infinite distance in the future, but cognizing the fact that duration not only is, but must be forever.

It is said that time cannot have a real existence; for then God, who cognizes all things, would cognize its existence: but with God there is no succession; all events are present to his view in an "eternal now." We can form no conception of an "eternal now." God views events as successive, because they are successive. His views must be in accordance with truth. He created things at different times; and he continues to act. Immutability does not prevent him from doing to-day what he did not do yesterday. He is the same to-day, yesterday, and forever—that is, his holy character remains unchanged. Character remains unchanged, though the acts that manifest it may vary and take place at different times.

The mode of the Divine existence, and of the action of the Divine Mind, is beyond our powers of cognition. Hence we should make no unauthorized or unmeaning assertions concerning it.

Duration is a reality. It is a fact that events take place as successive; that successiveness may be measured. Some writers say that time is a mere word expressive of the fact that events are successive. Suppose all events and all created objects were to cease— would there be any such thing as duration? God would endure. Is time, then, an attribute of God, as some have contended? The everlasting existence of God is a fact, but is no part of his being, as benevolence and justice are.

What then is time, or duration? The best answer that can be given is, that it is time, duration. We know what it is, though we cannot define it or state in what it consists.

We have all the knowledge of time that is needed. We must not, in order to carry out our notions of philosophical inquiry, multiply words without knowledge. In every department of knowledge the last resort is, the mind's cognition that a thing is; and all questions beyond that may be answered by saying, "I don't know." It often requires as much discrimination to make an intelligent confession of ignorance, as to make the clearest explanations.

Duration and space are infinite; that is, the one has limitless extension, and the other is without beginning or end. It has been said that if space and time are infinite realities, and God is an infinite Being, then we have three infinite existences—which, it is alleged, is impossible. It is not possible that there be three infinite beings, but there is no absurdity in supposing the existence of limitless space as the theatre of creative power for an infinite being, nor in supposing that that being has always lived, and always will live. We do not assume that infinite duration is an infinite being.

CHAPTER XV.

RELATIONS.

WHEN we cognize two or more objects, we cognize something more than their existence and qualities. When we cognize the pillars of a portico, we see that they are similar to each other. We look upon two adjacent mountains, and see that one is higher than the other. We see a number of men marching, and that one goes before the other. We see a blow given to a standing pillar, and it falls: the blow caused the pillar to fall.

In the above-mentioned cases we cognize the objects, and certain relations existing between them; we cognize the relations of resemblance, superiority, of antecedence and consequence, and of cause and effect.

No object, material or mental, exists isolated. The almost numberless existences have relations existing between them, and a knowledge of these relations constitutes no small part of our knowledge.

Existences and their relations may be said to constitute the entire material of our knowledge.

Some of the more obvious relations may easily be classified, such as those of resemblance, of proportion, and of cause and effect. The number of relations is so great, that an exhaustive classification cannot be made. The field of mental discovery—I do not mean as to the operations of mind, but as to truth—pertains chiefly to relations between known existences and truths. Relations exist not only between existing things, but between one another. Every thought sustains certain relations to other thoughts. The cognition of relations previously unnoticed, constitutes, to a good degree, originality of thought.

An original thinker does not create truth, any more than an original geographical discoverer creates the rivers and mountains which he makes known to the world. The man of original thought is one who sees more clearly and further than his fellows. Originality of thought is not then a sudden inspiration, it is simply mental seeing—seeing what is. The power may thus be cultivated. The sailor sharpens his vision by careful and earnest looking into the distant blending of the earth and sky, and hence can discern a sail long before it is visible to uneducated eyes. In like manner, some, by steady and earnest looking in the direction of truth, come to see objects unseen by others. Newton cultivated original thought by long and patient looking. All true originality is to be sought in that way, and not by imitating the uncouth phraseology of men claiming to possess originality.

The perception of relations has usually been treated as an act of judgment. If one chooses to call those cognitions which are the result of the cognition of two or more objects, judgments, it may be well, though there is danger of leading the indiscriminating reader to suppose a judgment to be something generically different from a cognition.

Judgment is said to be the result of comparison. The mind compares two objects, and judges that they are equal, or that one is greater than the other—that they agree or disagree. It is desirable to confine the word judgment to those opinions or beliefs which are the result of evidence made up of parts, each inconclusive in itself, or of evidences conflicting. Thus we say a man has sound judgment, whose opinions on difficult and complicated subjects are usually correct.

The operation of the mind in cognizing relations, seems to be this: We cognize the objects, and then the relation existing between them. Our cognitions of relations are conditioned upon our cognition of the objects related. This is what actually takes place; and nothing is gained, and much may be lost, by calling in the agency of the faculty of judgment.

Our knowledge of relations is as positive and real as our knowledge of existences. The mind does not create the resemblance between two objects; it simply cognizes it. The resemblance is a reality as truly as the resembling objects are a reality. The reality of the resemblance is not a reality apart from the resembling objects. There can be no such thing as resemblance apart from resembling objects. The fact that the objects resemble each other, is a real fact. Our knowledge which has relations for its subject, is thus as real as any portion of our knowledge.

Some relations are cognized intuitively, and others mediately, that is, by the aid of other truths. The relations existing between material and spiritual existences, and between all objects of thought and feeling, are inexhaustible to finite minds.

CHAPTER XVI.

RESEMBLANCE—GENERALIZATION—GENERAL TERMS—
ABSTRACT TERMS.

ONE of the most important of relations is that of resemblance. Our cognition of resemblance is said to be the result of comparison. It is said we compare the objects, and by an act of judgment perceive that they are like or unlike. What is the process as revealed by consciousness? I look toward a forest, and see two oaks, and also see that they are similar in size, form, and color. The perception of the trees is a direct act, and the perception of their resemblance follows the perception of the trees. If both the trees are within range of vision at the same moment, the perception of resemblance immediately follows the perception of the trees. It may be that the trees may not both be perceived at the same moment. An act of memory then takes place antecedent to the perception of resemblance. The perception of resemblance is a direct perception, conditioned on the perception of the trees. Comparison is not therefore an act generically different from an act of cognition.

Classification and generalization are conditioned on our power of cognizing resemblance. Our cognitions are always of particulars—are always individual cognitions. If we had not the power of classification, we should be overwhelmed with the number of individual objects, and language would fail us in our attempts to designate them. By classification we condense our knowledge, and make it manageable.

We have before us, in a park, a vast number of animals. We have never seen them before. Were our knowledge confined to individuals, it would soon become confused and unwieldy. But we notice that some resemble others, and we mentally separate those resembling each other in certain points, and put them in a class by themselves. We give to each class a name.

The process supposed is strictly analogous to the process of generalization. Objects resembling each other are placed in a class by themselves, and a name given to the class. The name thus given is a common or general term.

(Have general terms any meaning?) Are there any real existences corresponding to the terms animal, man, tree? There are individual animals, individual men, individual trees. Are there any such things as a general animal, a general man, a general tree? We can form a conception, idea, or notion of an individual animal—a bear, for instance; of an individual man—John, for instance; of an individual tree—the hickory that overshadowed the homestead. But can we form a conception or notion of a general man, a general animal, a general tree? If we make the attempt, shall we not find the notion of an individual as the result? Have general terms, then, no meaning? Are they merely names?

It may be said that general terms stand for all the individuals of the class—that man means all men. We must distinguish between general and collective terms. A collective term, such as army, congregation, church, includes the aggregate of individuals composing the army or the church. The amount of meaning of the term varies at different times. But not so with general terms. The meaning of the term man remains the same, whether there are more or fewer men. It is clear that it has some meaning, is not a mere name, and that there is no such thing as an existing man in general for it to signify. What, then, does it stand for? What is the object of our thoughts, when we employ a general term? The general term or name of a class expresses the qualities common to all the members of the class. Man stands for those qualities which belong to all men. We see that all men resemble each other in some respects, though they may differ in other respects. The term man, then, has a meaning as truly as the term John.

McCosh remarks: "It has been very generally allowed by philosophers, that the mind begins with the knowledge of individual objects or scenes presented to it. , Among these objects it may, by its comparative faculty, discover resemblances. In some cases the comparison is preceded by an abstraction of the qualities in respect of which the objects are alike; in other cases it may be perceived at once that there is a resemblance, and the abstraction of the points of resemblance may follow. In all cases, both the discovery of resemblance and abstraction are needful to generalization, in which we put in a class, and usually call by a common name, the objects thought to resemble each other in certain respects, and so far as they resemble each other.

"I am prepared to lay down, in regard to generalization, a proposition similar to that which I am inclined to enforce in regard to abstraction. When the individuals are real, the generalization has also a reality; that is, there is a reality in the class. True, I may constitute a class from imaginary individuals— say a class of griffins, or a class of mermaids, or a class of ghosts. In such a case the general is as unreal as the singular. But if my generalization is from real objects; if it is a generalization made up of objects in nature, say of marbles, or reptiles, or cruciferous plants, or even of objects of human workmanship, such as chairs, or houses, or churches, then the intellectual product has also a reality involved.

"I do not mean to say that the general exists, or can exist, as an individual thing, like the singulars which it embraces—that the class crocodile has the same sort of existence as the individual crocodile; but I maintain that it has a reality in the common attributes possessed by the objects.

"In abstraction, the reality may be simply that of an attribute in an individual object. In generalization, it is the possession of a common attribute by an indefinite number of objects. The composition of marble is a fact quite as much, though not exactly of the same sort, as the limestone itself. The possession of cold blood, and of the three heart-compartments, is a reality quite as much as the individual crocodile is. The possession of four cross petals is a real thing, just as a particular wild mustard plant is. The structure and adaptation to a practical use, of chair, house, and church, are not fictitious, any more than this chair, or this house, or this church is. This account preserves us, on the one hand, from an extravagant realism, which would give to the universal the same sort of reality as the singular; and, on the other, from an extreme conceptualism or nominalism, which would place the reality solely in the conception of the mind, or in the name. The class has a reality, but it is simply in the possession of common qualities by an indefinite number of objects.

"According to this view, abstraction and generalization are processes of a very high order; they are, in fact, essential to philosophy, quite as much so indeed, as Plato and the Schoolmen supposed. With out them we can never reach the truths on which the higher forms of wisdom gaze. They always presuppose, indeed, that something has been given them; but, acting upon this, they turn it to most important purposes; and if they start with realities and are properly conducted, they are ever in the region of realities, and of realities of the highest kind. We shall see, as we advance, that all philosophic notions and maxims are the results of these processes, some of them being abstractions, and others being also of the nature of generalizations."

Generalization is said to depend upon abstraction. There is connected with the latter term, at least in the minds of some, an obscurity which it may be well to dispel. The act of abstraction is not so difficult and mysterious as is sometimes supposed. We see an object—a rose, for example—and fix our attention exclusively upon the color. We perform an act of abstraction. To contemplate an object abstractly, is to make it an object of exclusive attention.

Abstract and general terms are often confounded. Abstract terms are expressive of our notion of qualities, attributes, or objects, viewed apart from the qualities, attributes, or objects with which they are connected. I see a round object—a globe. I can contemplate the roundness apart from the color and density of the ball. I say of the ball that it is round. The same quality which leads me to affirm that the ball is round, when contemplated apart from the ball, separated in thought from the ball, is called *roundness*. Is there any such thing as roundness? Not as a separate entity. Roundness is the name applied to a quality viewed apart from other qualities. It has, therefore, a real significance.

"Abstraction," says McCosh, "may be considered in a wider or in a narrower sense. It may be regarded, in an extended sense, as that operation of mind in which, to use the language of Whately, 'we draw off and contemplate separately any part of an object presented to the mind, disregarding the rest.' In this more general sense the parts may exist separately as well as the whole; thus, having seen a judge with his wig, we can not only separate in thought the wig from the judge, but the wig can in fact be separated from the wearer. In a narrower sense, abstraction is that operation of mind in which we contemplate the quality of an object separately from the object.

"'An abstract name,' says Mr. Mill ('Logic,' book i. ch. ii.), 'is a name which stands for an attribute of a thing.' In this sense, the part separated in thought cannot be separated from the object in fact. Color may be thought of (not seen or imagined) apart from an extended body, but cannot exist apart from a colored object.

"It is a common impression that our abstractions are in no sense realities. I wish, at this early stage of the investigations to be prosecuted in this treatise, to set myself against this view which has sometimes been positively expressed, but is far more frequently underlying and implied in statements and arguments without being formally announced. I lay down a very different position, that if the concrete be real, and the abstraction be properly made, the abstract thing, that is, the thing contemplated in the abstraction, will also be real. I may never have seen a bird without wings, but I can consider the wings apart from the bird, and I am sure that the wings have as real an existence as the bird itself. This will be admitted at once in regard to all such cases as this, in which I can in fact separate the pinions from the body of the fowl. But I go a step further, and maintain, that even in cases in which the part abstracted cannot be separated in reality from the whole, still it is to be considered as real. It may not have, or be capable of having, an independent reality, but still it has a reality. I can think of gravitation apart from a given body, or from the chemical affinity of that body; and in doing so I do not suppose that it can exist apart from body; still the gravitation has an existence just as much as the body has: it has not a reality independent of the body, but it has a reality in the body, as a quality of it. The same remark might be applied to, and will hold good of, any other abstraction. No doubt, if the original concrete object be imaginary, the abstraction formed from it may be the same. I can separate in thought the beauty of Venus from Venus herself;

and, of course, as Venus is ideal, so also is her beauty. But when the object is real, and I abstract or separately contemplate what has been known in the real, then, as the concrete object is real, so is also the part or quality abstracted real; not that it may be a reality capable of subsisting in itself, but still a reality in the object as a quality of it.

"I reckon it of the utmost moment to make this remark. The view here presented saves us, on the one hand, from an extreme realism, which would attribute an independent reality to every quality abstracted—which would, for example, represent beauty as a separate thing, like a beautiful scene in nature; and, on the other hand, from what is more important in our present inquiry, from regarding it as a nonentity, or at the utmost as a mere form or creation of the mind. We are ever hearing the phrase repeated, a 'mere abstraction;' and the language is applied to such objects as space, time, beauty, and even truth and moral good. In opposition to such views, I maintain that abstraction is not necessarily concerned about fictions or illusions. Abstractions are not, as they have often been represented, the attenuated ghosts of departed quantities; they may rather be represented as the very skeleton of the body, not capable of action alone, but still an important existence in the body, acting with its covering of flesh and skin."

In former times, the question, "What is the object of thought when we employ general terms?" was a prolific subject of discussion.

The Nominalists held that general terms are mere names without any signification—that we have no ideas corresponding to general terms. The Realists held that there are real existences corresponding to those terms.

Nominalism is still held by quite a number of philosophers: a modified style of realism seems also to be held by some.

We have seen what general terms signify. It may be well to notice a statement made by nominalists. It is said that we can form no general idea of any class of objects: we can form only particular ideas. We can form an idea of an acute-angled triangle, and of a right-angled triangle, and of an obtuse-angled triangle; but we cannot form an idea of a general triangle which shall be acute, right, obtuse, and right-angled at the same time.

In this statement the term idea is used as synonymous with image. We cannot form a mental image of an acute, obtuse, and right-angled triangle in one. It should be observed that a fact may be real, though not mentally picturable. The general term may have a meaning, though that meaning may not constitute a mental image.

. The general term triangle includes the qualities in which the different kinds of triangle agree. They agree in having three sides and three angles.

No one affirms that the general term stands for any and every kind of triangle in particular, as the objection above stated assumes. It stands for those things which are common to all triangles.

Bailey denies altogether the existence of abstract ideas or notions. "It has been maintained by eminent philosophers, that we form in our minds what they term abstract notions corresponding to the abstract terms employed in writing and speaking; but they have not been hitherto successful in their attempts to show what an abstract notion is. On closely analyzing what passes in my own mind, I do not discover that I can think of any thing but particular objects and events, either apart or combined, single or numerous, with various degrees of distinctness or completeness."

Again: "Now, my doctrine is, that, as we are unable to perceive, so we are unable to conceive any separate entity corresponding to an abstract term; nor are we conscious of any peculiar mental phenomena to which that term can be applied. In different language, we have no ideas in the mind answering to such words as extension and motion; but when they are used, we think of an extended and moving body. Our thoughts on such occasions may frequently be vague, shadowy, indistinct, and fugitive, but their real character is what I have described it to be."

Because the term brightness suggests the thought

of the sun, or a lamp, or some other bright object, Bailey affirms that it has no meaning—that is, "no notion corresponding to it;" that there are "no peculiar mental phenomena to which it can be applied."

We affirm that it expresses a quality considered apart from the object to which it belongs, and that this is the peculiar mental phenomenon to which it is properly applied. Bright expresses a quality belonging to some object. Brightness expresses the quality mentally viewed as separate from the object. Brightness is not an entity separate from a material object. It marks a quality of a material object contemplated in a particular way. Brightness, truth, life, denote no separate entities, but qualities of objects, propositions, beings, viewed abstractly. The abstract term does not express an existence, but a mental phenomenon which is as real as any existence.

The fact that an abstract or general term brings up with greater or less distinctness a particular image, does not prove that said image is the signification of the term. When you speak of the house in which you live, the image of the house arises, and of the overhanging tree also. But the tree is no part of the idea of the house.

General terms and abstract terms, then, are not mere words. They do not express entities apart from the individuals of the class, and the substance. They do not express nonentities, but realities such as have been described above.

Individual terms are more definite and precise than general and abstract terms. In composition, vivacity is promoted by avoiding as much as may be the use of abstract, general, and collective terms. The fact that our original cognitions are individual, gives a hint as to the best mode of producing cognitions in the minds of others.

CHAPTER XVII.

CAUSE AND EFFECT.

EVENTS have various relations existing between them. The most important one is that of cause and effect.

Every physical event has a cause. We may be ignorant of the cause of a given event—we may fail to discover it even after the most careful investigation; but we know that the event had a cause. What is the ground of this knowledge?

We will suppose the event to be the fall of a tree: what is the ground of our knowledge of that event? We saw it—we saw the tree fall; that is, the mind cognized the fact through the sense of sight.

What is the ground of our knowledge that the event thus cognized had a cause? The same as our knowledge of the event: we saw it—not the particular cause of the event, but saw that it had a cause.

We know that an event has a cause just as we know that the event occurs. In both cases we cognize the fact. Whenever we cognize an event, we also cognize the fact that it had a cause. Both are direct, intuitive cognitions of the mind. In the one case, the cognition may take place through the agency of the senses; in the other case, the cognition is conditioned on the cognition of the event.

Perhaps it may be said, in answer to the question, How do we know that every event has a cause? that we know it from experience. If by this is meant, that in the case of every event cognized by us, we have cognized the fact that it had some cause, the assertion is true. But the idea of cause is no more the result of experience, than the idea of the event is the result of experience. Cognitions of both are experiences, but not deductions from former experiences.

The truth of the proposition, every event has a cause, is not the result of experience in the sense in which the expression is commonly used. We say we learn from experience that men are to be tried before they are trusted. The conclusion is the result of numerous cognitions. No single cognition would authorize the conclusion. We learn from experience that all kinds of wood will burn—not that we have burned all kinds of wood: we have burned several kinds, and hence conclude that all kinds of wood will burn.

We do not come to the conclusion that every event has a cause, because we have found that a number of events have had causes, and hence conclude that all must have. The truth that all events

6*

must have causes is cognized as soon as an event is cognized. When we have cognized a thousand events, no additional certainty is thereby added to the proposition. We are certain of its truth when we have cognized one event.

No one, on consulting his past consciousness, will find that he was once ignorant of the truth that every event must have a cause—that is, ignorant after he had cognized an event—and that he acquired that truth gradually by experience.

The infant gives evidence that it cognizes this truth as soon as it cognizes events. It also cognizes the kindred proposition that like causes produce like effects. Let him burn his fingers in the flame of a candle, and he will not thrust them into the flame a second time.

The maxim, every event must have a cause, is a generalized statement of what we intuitively cognize whenever we cognize an event.

The following is McCosh's method of showing that our cognition of causality is not a generalization from experience:

"First, it would not, as being the result of generalization, operate at so early a period of life as our belief in cause and effect evidently does. The causal belief [cognition] is as strong in infancy as in mature life or in old age; is as strong among savages as in civilized countries in which scientific observation has made the greatest advances. True, savage nations have not a belief in the uniformity of nature, which is a result of observation; they discover events which are thought to have no cause in nature, but then they seek for a cause beyond nature. Now, if the conviction of causation were like the belief in the uniformity of nature, a principle derived from induction—which must necessarily be a large induction—it would be difficult to account for its existence and its invariable operation in the earliest stages of individual life and of society. I admit that all this merely proves that there is a native instinct or inclination prompting us to rise from an effect to a cause, and by no means justifies us in standing up for a necessary conviction.

"Secondly, it would scarcely account for the universality of the belief of men brought up in such various countries and situations, attached to such different sects and creeds, and under the influence of all kinds of whim and caprice. This can be most satisfactorily explained by supposing that there is a native principle at work, inclining and guiding all men. Such a consideration, I allow, does not show that the conviction is a fundamental one, nor would I urge it as in itself a positive proof of the existence even of a native instinct; still it is a strong presumption. Indeed, the theory which supposes that there is some original impulse or inclination, is the only one which can give a full explanation of all the beliefs which man cherishes, and the judgments which he ever pronounces.

"Thirdly, it would not account for the fundamental and necessary character of the judgment. This is the conclusive circumstance, of which the others are to be regarded as merely corroborations. No possible length or uniformity could or should give this necessity of conviction to the judgment. We might have seen A and B, this stone and that stone, this star and that star, this man and that man together, a thousand, or a million, or a billion of times, and without our ever having seen them separate; but this would not and ought not to necessitate us to believe that they have been forever together, and shall be forever together, and must be forever together. No doubt, it would lead us when we fell in with the one to look for the other, and we would wonder if the one presented itself without the other; still, it is possible for us to conceive, and, on evidence being produced, to believe that there may be the one without the other. It was long supposed that all metals are comparatively heavy; but while every one was astonished at the fact, no one was prepared to deny it, when it was shown by Davy that potassium floated on water. Down to a very recent date civilized men had never seen a black swan, yet no naturalist was ever so presumptuous as to affirm that there never could be such an animal; and when black swans were discovered in Australia, scientific men, no doubt, wondered, but never went so far as to deny the fact. A very wide and uniform experience would justify a general expectation, but not a necessary conviction; and this experience is liable to be disturbed at any time by a new occurrence inconsistent with what has been previously known to us. But the belief in the connection between cause and effect is of a totally different character. We can believe that two things which have been united since creation began, may never be united again while creation lasts; but we never can be made to believe, or rather think, judge, or decide (for this is the right expression), that a change can take place without a cause. We can believe that night and day might henceforth be disconnected, and that from and after this day or some other day there would only be perpetual day or perpetual night on the earth; but we could never be made to decide that, the causes which produced day and night being the same, there ever could be any other effect than day and night. We could believe, on sufficient evidence, that the sun might not rise on our earth to-morrow; but we never could be made to judge that, the sun and earth and all other things necessary to the sun rising on our earth abiding as they are, the luminary of day should not run his round as usual. We see at once that there is a difference between the judgment of the mind in the two cases; in the case in which we have before us a mere conjunction sanctioned by a wide and invariable induction, and that in which we have an effect, and connect it with its cause. The one belief can be overcome, and should be overcome at any time by a new inconsistent fact coming under our observation; whereas, in regard to the other, we are confident that it never can be modified or set aside, and we feel that it ought not to be overborne."

Mr. J. S. Mill, the author of Mill's "Logic" and other very able works, denies that the cognition of "the law of causation" is intuitive. He regards the proposition that every event has a cause as true, so far as this world is concerned, because observation has shown it to be true.

"The uniformity in the succession of events," he remarks, " otherwise called the law of causation, must not be received as a law of the universe, but of that portion of it only that is within range of our sure observation, with a reasonable degree of extension to adjacent cases."

Again: "I am convinced that any one accustomed to abstraction and analysis, who will fairly exert his faculties for the purpose, will, when his imagination has learned to entertain the notion, find no difficulty in conceiving that in some one, for instance, of the many firmaments into which sidereal astronomy now divides the universe, events may succeed one another at random without any fixed law; nor can any thing in our experience, or in our mental nature, constitute a sufficient, or indeed any reason for believing that this is nowhere the case."

If by "events succeeding one another at random," he means happening without a cause, then our "mental nature" does furnish a sufficient reason for denying his assertion. The mind is so constituted that it cognizes the fact that distant events must have causes, as well as those which are near at hand.

If he means to assert that a different kind of uniformity may exist in other portions of the universe, the assertion may be correct. Different causes may exist in different portions of the universe. The uniformity which we witness may not prevail throughout the universe; but the truth that every event has a cause does thus prevail.

If it be asked, How do we know that an event in Sirius must have a cause? the reply is, the mind cognizes that truth. If it be asked, How can the mind cognize a truth so distant from it? the reply is, the mind does cognize said truth. The questions, *How* can the mind cognize? and *what* does it cognize? are distinct. We can answer the latter, but not the former.

Dr. Thomas Brown taught that invariable antecedence and consequence constitutes the relation of cause and effect. He affirms that "we have no other idea in our minds when we speak of cause and effect, than an invariable antecedence and consequence."

If antecedence and consequence constitute the

relation of cause and effect, there is no such thing as power. The terms power, efficacy, energy, mean nothing but invariable antecedence and consequence.

"To him," says this author, "who had previously kindled a fire, and placed on it a vessel full of water, with a certainty that in that situation the water would become speedily hot, what additional information would be given by telling him that the fire had the power of boiling water?"

"It is only by confounding casual with uniform and invariable antecedence, that power can be conceived to be something different from antecedence."

"In the various changes that occur, there can as little be any powers or susceptibilities different from the antecedents and consequents themselves, as there can be forms differing from the coexisting particles of matter which constitute them."

In opposition to these assertions, it is sufficient to say that all men do cognize the existence of power in the antecedents which are causes. Words expressive of the idea of power are found in every language. All men testify to the fact that they intuitively cognize the existence of power. If they, like Brown, deny it in words, their actions testify to the truth.

There are many things invariably antecedent to other things, which are not the causes of those things. The antecedent which has power to produce the consequent, is the antecedent which we cognize as the cause.

"Simple and invariable succession," says Dr. Hickok, "is not our conviction of cause and effect, nor at all like it. Night invariably succeeds the day; one o'clock invariably succeeds twelve o'clock; one fixed star invariably succeeds another fixed star in crossing our meridian; but none of these invariable successions is our conviction of causal connection. If we assume two pair of wheels, one of which has each wheel separately driven so that the cogs in their periphery exactly match in every revolution; but the other pair is so constructed, that one wheel being moved, its cogs drive the other; there will be alike invariable succession in each case; but we must carry the mind quite beyond the fact of invariable succession to some efficiency in an antecedent that produces the consequent. No conception of simple succession, no matter how invariable, is our notion of cause."

The consciousness of the reader will attest the truth of the statement thus made.

The following remarks are from the pen of Professor Wilson, Dr. Brown's successor in the chair of Moral Philosophy at Edinburgh. They are given as quoted by Hamilton. The test proposed by Dr. Brown was: "Let any one ask himself what it is which he means by the term power, and, without contenting himself with a few phrases which signify nothing, reflect before he gives his answer, and he will find that he means nothing more than that, in all similar circumstances, the explosion of gunpowder will be the immediate and uniform consequence of the application of a spark."

"Let us, then," says Professor Wilson, "apply the test by which Dr. Brown proposes the truth of his views shall be tried. Let us ask ourselves what we mean when we say that the spark has power to kindle the gunpowder—that powder is susceptible of being kindled by the spark. Do we mean only, that when they come together this will happen? Do we merely predict this visible and certain futurity?

"We do not fear to say, that when we speak of a power in one substance to produce a change in another, and of a susceptibility of such change in that other, we express more than our belief that the change has taken place, and will take place. There is more in our mind than a conviction of the past and a foresight of the future. There is, besides this, the conception of a fixed constitution of their nature, which determines the event—a constitution which, while it lasts, makes the event the necessary consequence of the situation in which the objects are placed. We should say, then, that there are included in these terms, 'power' and 'susceptibility of change,' two ideas which are not expressed in Dr. Brown's analysis—one of necessity, and the other of a constitution of things, in which that necessity is established. That these two ideas are not expressed in Dr. Brown's analysis, is seen by quoting again his words: 'He will find that he means nothing more than that, in all similar circumstances, the explosion of gunpowder will be the immediate and uniform consequence of the application of a spark.'

"It is certain, from the whole tenor of his work, that Dr. Brown has designed to exclude the idea of necessity from his analysis."

The following is Dr. Hickok's account of Kant's view of the relation of cause and effect:

"Kant assumes the phenomenal consequences to be real; but what the substances as things in themselves, of which these phenomena are only qualities, truly are, can never be known by human intelligence. The mind, as a regulative principle of its thinking in judgments, is obliged to use the conception of causality, and bring its sequences into connection under this category; but this notion of causality is altogether subjective—a mental conception for regulating the mind's own thinking; and we cannot say that the phenomenal realities have any such connections in the things themselves. The mind has such original forms, as pure conceptions, from itself, and, in thinking, it fits these forms on to the real phenomena, and brings them into orderly connection thereby; but it is the mind which makes the connections, and not that the connections are in the things themselves, and that they make the mind to know after their conditions."

Kant admits that we have the idea of power, but

affirms that it is simply " subjective "—a figment of the mind, not a cognition of reality. Consciousness attests that the idea of power is the cognition of a reality in things themselves.

Sir William Hamilton has put forth a new theory of causality; we presume his claims to originality in regard to it are just.

The following is his account of " the phenomenon of causality": " When we are aware of something which begins to be, we are, by the necessity of our intelligence, constrained to believe that it has a cause. But what does the expression, *that it has a cause*, signify? If we analyze our thought, we shall find that it simply means that, as we cannot conceive any new existence to commence, therefore all that is now seen to arise under a new appearance had previously an existence under a prior form. We are utterly unable to realize in thought the possibility of the complement of existence being either increased or diminished. We are unable, on the one hand, to conceive of nothing becoming something, or, on the other hand, of something becoming nothing. When God is said to create out of nothing, we construe this to thought by supposing that He evolves existence out of Himself. We view the Creator as the cause of the universe. *Ex nihilo nihil, in nihilum nil posse reverti*, expresses, in its purest form, the whole intellectual phenomenon of causality." He affirms " that causation is simply our inability to think an absolute commencement or an absolute termination of being."

If causation is simply our inability to think an absolute commencement or an absolute termination of being, it is wholly a subjective matter. But it is to be presumed that he meant that our idea of cause is the result of our inability. The question is not to be decided by an inference from an elaborate theory of "the conditioned," or from any other theory, but by an appeal to consciousness. Whenever an event takes place, does not every one intuitively cognize the truth that it had an adequate cause? Is not the cognition of cause as clear and defined a cognition, as any cognition of which we are conscious? May we not as well say that our cognition of a body as extended or colored is the result of "inability," as our cognition of cause? If it be a fact of consciousness, that whenever we cognize an event we intuitively cognize the fact that it must have an adequate cause, then the elaborate theory of Hamilton is false.

Some questions may be asked with respect to Hamilton's statements as to the phenomena of causality. Is it true that "all that is now seen to arise under a new appearance, had previously an existence under a prior form"? In what form did the material universe exist, before God "in the beginning created the heavens and the earth"? Will it be said that it existed in the power of God? That is simply saying that God had power to bring it into existence.

Is it true that we cannot conceive of God creating something out of nothing; and that we construe it to thought by supposing that He evolves existence out of Himself? We cannot, it is granted, conceive how God creates something out of nothing; but we can conceive the fact of His doing so.

What is meant by evolving existence out of Himself? Is it affirmed that the world previously existed in God? If it existed as matter, is God then material? If it existed as spirit, then can spirit be changed into matter?

Can any thing be properly said to be evolved from the Divine existence in any other sense than that of being created by Divine power? If this is what Hamilton means, then his view of causation is reduced to the one received practically by all men, and his claims to the discovery amount simply to a new use of terms.

It has by some been thought difficult to account for the character of necessity which attaches to our idea of cause. When we see an event, we not only see that it has a cause, but that it must have a cause.

We see that a cause is necessary because it is necessary, just as we see that a raven is black because it is black. That every event *must* have a cause, is a truth which the human mind can cognize; that the raven is black, is also a truth which the human mind can cognize; and there is no more difficulty or mystery in the one case than in the other.

The law or fact of causation is sometimes inaccurately stated, and needless difficulties have thus been caused. "As the doctrine of causation is sometimes stated," says McCosh, "it might appear as if we were required, in following the chain of cause and effect, to go back *ad infinitum*. It is said in a loose way, that every object must have a cause; and then, as this cause must also have a cause, it might seem as if we were compelled to go on forever from one link to another. In particular, it might appear as if we could never legitimately argue from the law of causation in favor of this world being caused; for, if the law of cause and effect be universal, then we must seek for a cause, not only of the world, but of the Being who made the world; and if it be not universal, then it is conceivable that this world may be one of the things that are not caused. This is an objection urged with great confidence by Kant; and a large school of metaphysicians seem to think that it is fatal to any argument in favor of the Divine existence derived from human intelligence, as in every such argument the law of causation must enter as an element. Kant endeavors to escape from the dismal consequences in which he felt himself being engulfed, by declaring that the law of cause and effect, which thus required an infinite *regressus*, was a law of thought and not of things, and by calling in a moral argument (which argument has again been assailed by the very objections which Kant directed against the speculative argument; for if our intelligence be a delusion, why may not our moral convictions also be so?); while a large body of thinkers appealed to some sort of mysterious faith which will not submit to be examined, or even expressed. But, with all deference to these bold asseverations, I maintain that if only this cosmos can be shown to bear marks of being an effect, the argument from causation can carry us up to a supermundane cause, while it does not require us to go back to a cause of that cause. All inquiry into causation conducts us to substance; but it does not compel us to go on further, or to go on forever. The law of causality does insist that the world, as an effect, must have a cause in a Being possessing power; and if, on inquiring into the nature of that Being, we have reason to believe that He or it must be an effect, it would insist on our going on to look out for a further cause. But if, on the other hand, we find no signs of that Being who made the world being an effect, our intuition regarding causation would be entirely satisfied in looking on that Being as uncaused, as self-existent, as having power in Himself. It thus appears that this difficulty, which has puzzled so many, has arisen entirely from a misapprehension and perversion of the law of causation, commencing with Hume, and presented in a new form by Kant."

Nearly allied to the maxim, Every event must have an adequate cause, is the maxim, Like causes produce like effects. This principle lies at the foundation of our belief in the uniformity of the course of nature. Some of the Scotch philosophers refer our belief in the uniformity of nature to an original principle. Reid says: " God hath implanted in human minds an original principle, by which we believe and expect the continuance of those connections which we have observed in times past."

This is a very incautious statement. If the human mind is made to believe that the course of nature is uniform—that is, if this belief is original and instinctive—then the human mind cannot believe a miracle, however well attested, since a miracle is a deviation from the uniform course of nature. If this principle be implanted in the minds of all men, it will be found in the minds of those who shall live when the world's history is about to be closed. Hence they will be led by a divinely implanted principle to believe what is not true !

It is a self-evident truth, that the same or similar causes, under the same or similar conditions, will produce the same or similar effects. Hence, so long as the present causes are in operation, the course of nature will be uniform. · When new causes come into operation, changes will take place. We have observed that events have followed each other with a certain uniformity, and hence we infer that, so long as present causes continue to operate, events will succeed each other with a like uniformity. We expect causes to remain as they are, till we have some reason to suppose that there will be a change.

CHAPTER XVIII.

COGNITION OF BEAUTY.

THE mind can cognize beauty. We turn our eyes in winter toward the trunk and leafless branches of a tree; we cognize its existence and form. We turn our eyes in spring toward the tree in full bloom, and we cognize the additional fact that it is beautiful. We turn our eyes upward in a clear night: we cognize the fact that the stars studding the blue vault are beautiful. We hear a strain of music, and cognize the fact that it is beautiful. We witness an act of self-sacrificing affection, and cognize the fact that it is beautiful. We cognize objects that are useful, objects that are injurious, and objects that are beautiful. Our cognitions of beauty are as distinct from our cognitions of the useful, as are our cognitions of the injurious.

Beauty appertains to objects animate and inanimate, material and spiritual; to feelings, thoughts, and actions. It would be as impossible to make an exhaustive enumeration of beautiful objects, as to make an exhaustive enumeration of true propositions.

How do we know that the objects we call beautiful, are beautiful? Just as we know that the propositions we call true, are true. We know that the mind has power to cognize truth and beauty, because it does cognize truth and beauty. When we perceive the rainbow, we perceive its beauty. We have a direct, intuitive cognition of the beauty of many objects. In regard to every kind of knowledge, we must rely upon our primary cognitions, or we are at once without any ground of certainty. If things are not as we cognize them to be, then there is an end to all knowledge. Universal skepticism is the result.

The human mind is not infallible. It may err in its cognitions. One may think a proposition to be true when it is not, and one may think an object beautiful when it is not. But there are propositions relating both to truth and beauty, in regard to which he is not liable to err. There are intuitive cognitions which are certain. How do we know them to be certainly true? We cognize the fact; and we must rely upon the cognition, or fall into universal skepticism. Because the mind may err in certain cognitions, it does not follow that it may err in regard to all cognitions.

Beauty, as we have seen, is varied, as well as truth; that is, there are various things that are beautiful, and various things that are true. In what one thing do these diversified beautiful objects agree? The only answer that can be given to this question is, that they agree in being beautiful. The idea of beauty is a simple idea, and cannot be analyzed.

Writers have nevertheless attempted to analyze it, and to discover in what beauty consists. Different qualities or facts have been named by different writers as constituting *the* beautiful. The qualities thus set forth belong to some beautiful objects, but not to all. "Some have thought," says Cousin, "to find the beautiful in proportion; and this is, in fact, one of the conditions of beauty, but it is not the only one." * * * "What makes the terrible beauty of a storm? what makes that of a great picture, of an isolated verse, or a sublime ode?" The remark above quoted applies to all attempts to state in what the beautiful consists.

In truth, there is no such thing as the beautiful apart from beautiful objects. Beauty is not an independent entity. It is a quality of objects, and of relations between objects. Beauty is a general term, standing for that in which all beautiful objects agree; just as truth is a general term, standing for that in which all true propositions agree.

Cousin affirms: "Truth, beauty, and goodness are attributes, not entities. Now, there is no attribute without a subject. And as here the question is concerning absolute truth, beauty, and goodness, their substance can be nothing else but the absolute Being. It is thus we arrive at God."

Has Cousin come any nearer telling us what beauty

is, than those who say it consists in proportion? To affirm that beauty is an attribute of God, is simply to affirm that God is beautiful. When we say wisdom is an attribute of God, we simply affirm that God is wise—we do not explain what wisdom is. It may safely be affirmed that the Divine character is beautiful; but that is not explaining in what beauty consists.

Professor Haven affirms that "The true, the beautiful, and the good exist as simple, absolute, eternal principles. They are in the Divine mind. They are in the Divine works. They are in a sense independent of Deity. He does not create them. He cannot reverse or change their nature. He works according to them. They are not created by, but only manifested in what God does."

Is this a successful attempt to tell us what beauty is? It is, according to our author, the manifestation of a simple, absolute, eternal principle existing in the Divine mind. Is it certain that there is any information contained in these words? What kind of a principle is this principle of beauty? Wherein does it differ from the principle of truth? What proof is there that the principle of beauty is a simple, absolute, and eternal principle in the Divine mind, any more than the principle of form, or of extension?

It is said that beauty is the manifestation of the Divine nature. It is true, and so are all God's works the manifestation of His nature—of His character;

that is, they show what He is. We have no reason to suppose that beauty is, in a peculiar sense, the manifestation of the Divine nature. God is the author of all created beauty; but the fact that God has created a thing does not prove that it is identical in nature with Him; *i. e.*, that it is a part of Himself. He created matter, but matter is no part of the Divine nature.

It is useless to attempt to say what beauty and truth are, except by saying that they are beauty and truth. Attempts to go beyond this, and to affirm that they are principles in the Divine mind, convey no definite ideas, and have a pantheistic tendency.

It may not be amiss to notice in this connection the not infrequent expression, "God is the principle of truth." What is the meaning of the expression? Is it that He is the author and source of all truth? Did He create space and its relations, and originate the difference between right and wrong? Was there ever a time when the difference between right and wrong did not exist? Will it be said that "his Being embraces all truth"? Is it not proper to ask for the meaning of that expression?

Christ is said to be the truth; but that does not mean that truth and the Divine existence are the same. God is said to be love; but love and the Divine existence are not the same. God is also said to be a consuming fire; but a consuming fire and the Divine existence are not the same.

Christ is said to be the truth, because the truths relating to him are to man the most important of all truths. In comparison with the truths which are able to make us wise unto salvation, all scientific and political truths are of little value.

These remarks in regard to the principle of truth, apply in all respects to the principle of beauty.

It is affirmed by some that all beauty is the expression of mental qualities. There is a beauty of expression. A countenance whose features are plain, not to say ugly, beams with an expression of benevolence, and is therefore beautiful. A delicate lily is beautiful. It suggests the idea of woman's delicacy and purity. It is remotely analogous to woman's delicacy and purity. A distinction is to be made between the signs of a thing and an analogy between two things. We have found from experience that certain things signify the presence of other things. We have also found that certain things are analogous. This distinction is overlooked by those who would refer all beauty to expression.

Much of the beauty of the human countenance is the beauty of expression, and depends, not on the form and coloring of the features, but upon the condition of the mind. The condition of the indwelling mind will give expression to the countenance. One cannot change the structure of his features, but he can change the condition of his mind. Let him aim to form a beautiful mind, and so far as he succeeds, it will appear in the expression of his countenance and person.

Association has a great influence on our opinions in regard to beauty. It has, in some instances, power to reverse our ideas as to the beauty of an object. An object, an article of dress, for example, when first seen by us, may appear to us the reverse of beautiful; but when we have seen it worn by those whose opinions we are accustomed to respect—when it has become the fashion—we come to regard it as beautiful. In consequence of association, some objects are regarded in some countries as beautiful, which are regarded as ugly in other countries. In consequence of the diversities of opinion in regard to beauty, caused by association, some have referred all beauty to association. They deny that there is any such thing as intrinsic beauty—that there are any objects originally adapted to produce ideas of beauty. They affirm that the power now possessed by some objects to awaken in our minds ideas and emotions of beauty, is wholly owing to association.

To such it is sufficient to say, that association will account for the transfer of the idea of beauty from one object to another, but cannot account for the origin of the idea. The idea of beauty must either be innate, or some object must have an original adaptation to produce it; that is, there must be some object beautiful in itself.

Association controls oftentimes our opinions of

beauty, but never controls our intuitive cognitions of beauty. There are objects whose beauty all men cognize intuitively. The rainbow, the flower of bright hues, the stars, are regarded as beautiful by all who have the ordinary attributes of humanity. When we pass from the sphere of intuition, and proceed to form judgments, opinions, on matters pertaining to beauty, we are liable to err, as in regard to all other subjects. Hence diversities of opinion in regard to beauty exist, just as diversities of opinion in regard to government exist. This does not prove that beauty is wholly subjective, and that one man's judgments are as good as another's. There are truths relating to beauty, just as there are truths relating to numbers; that is, there are truths æsthetic and truths mathematical. The mind's modes of procedure in cognizing these kinds of truth are similar. It cognizes some truths intuitively, and others by the aid of truths previously known.

All men possess the power of cognizing beauty; but all men do not possess this power in the same degree. All men can cognize mathematical truth, but some men can cognize it with greater clearness and rapidity than others.

The actual differences among men as to their power of cognizing beauty are owing to two causes. There is an original difference in the structure of their minds. Some men have by nature a keener sense of beauty than others. Then some men have the power of perceiving beauty more fully developed by education—by the education of instruction or the education of circumstances.

There is a greater difference among men in their power of perceiving beauty than in their power of perceiving truth—especially truth in relation to practical matters. Men are compelled by circumstances to exercise their powers in perceiving truth more than in perceiving beauty. Hence the power of perceiving truth is more fully developed.

The cognition of beauty is not a sensational cognition. By smell and taste we have, or may have, agreeable sensations. By the eye and ear we cognize beauty, which cognition is followed by or attended with a peculiar emotion, separable in thought from the cognition. An agreeable sensation—that is, an agreeable feeling localized in some part of the body—is one thing; an emotion, such as the emotion of beauty—a purely mental act—is another. The feeling of beauty, if the expression be allowed, is not a sensational feeling. When we look at the heavens or the waving wheat field, or listen to the æolian harp, the enjoyment is not localized in the eye and ear. The enjoyment is as purely mental as that resulting from perceiving a neat demonstration in geometry.

The emotion of beauty is a simple emotion, which cannot be described or analyzed, and can be known only by being felt. It is conditioned on the cognition of a beautiful object, or the presence of the idea of beauty in the mind. If we choose to call the mind's power of cognizing and enjoying beauty the æsthetic faculty, the acts of said faculty may be regarded as complex—composed of a cognition and an emotion.

Minds are differently constituted as to power to perform the different elements of this complex act. In some the perceptive and in others the emotive element predominates. Some men have clearer and more discriminative perceptions of beauty, and others have a deeper susceptibility in view of it.

Is there a standard of beauty, or of taste—an æsthetic yard-stick—something with which we compare objects, and judge them to be beautiful or not, according as they agree or disagree with it? Is every cognition of beauty a judgment, the result of comparison?

Some of our cognitions of beauty are direct, intuitive, and hence do not involve the process of comparison. In such cases, there can be no reference to a standard. Some of our cognitions are conditioned upon other cognitions, and may be said to be the result of comparison; that is, the process of comparison is among the conditions of the cognition. But in these cases there is no one idea or standard with which the object in question is compared.

There is what may be called a practical standard of taste, by which all are in some degree influenced. The books, statues, pictures, and edifices which have received the approbation and admiration of all cultivated minds, form a practical standard of taste. When a new work appears, we often unconsciously compare it with works of established reputation, and form our judgment accordingly.

While a due regard should be paid to authority, it should not be allowed to interfere with the formation of independent literary judgments; nor should one's freshness and originality be impaired by a too scrupulous conformity to the models furnished by standard authors and artists.

God designed that men should perceive and enjoy beauty. This appears from the fact that He has been profuse in the creation of beauty, and has given man capacity to perceive and enjoy it. Hence it is man's duty to cultivate his power of cognizing beauty.

It is cultivated by exercise. The choicest specimens of beauty in nature and art should be studied, that the mind's power of cognizing beauty may be improved.

The wise artist does not study his model that he may practise a servile imitation. He studies it to heighten his sense of the beautiful—that is, to improve his power of perceiving beauty—that he may form higher conceptions which he may strive to realize.

The study of beauty has a tendency to refine and ennoble the mind. Rightly conducted, it is favorable to morals, though there is no necessary connection between a fine taste and good morals. They have often been dissociated. There have been men of fine taste and of corrupt morals. Their corrupt morals were not the consequence of their fine taste. Whatever elevates the mind tends to good morals, though that tendency may be counteracted by other causes.

Our Puritan fathers erred in dissociating beauty from religion. In avoiding the Romish idolatry of worshipping the beautiful, they went to the opposite extreme. Hence the absence of all decoration in their places of worship, and the formation of a character in which the æsthetic element was sadly wanting. God's works are beautiful, and hence man's works dedicated to God's service should be beautiful. "Beauty and strength are in thy sanctuary." There is a beauty of holiness which, in one sense, includes all other beauty. God's children should not ignore the beauty which their Father has taken so much pains to create.

There are certain emotions that are sometimes called emotions of taste. These are the emotions of beauty, grandeur, sublimity, and the ludicrous. The emotion of grandeur is nearly allied to the emotion of beauty. An object which has none of the elements of beauty would scarcely be called a grand object. An object may be sublime without being at all beautiful.

All the emotions of taste are simple emotions,

and can be known only from experience. The emotion of sublimity is more intense and transient than the emotion of beauty. There are fewer objects in nature, and fewer thoughts, that awaken it. There are more beautiful than sublime writers.

Is there any such thing as sublimity apart from the emotion? The emotion is always preceded by a cognition or conception as its cause, and we call the object of that cognition or conception sublime. In what the sublimity of objects consists, cannot be told. There are certain objects that are sublime because they produce a certain effect on our minds. In some cases this effect may be owing to association; but there must be some objects originally adapted to produce the emotion, or we could never have it. We give the name of sublimity to that in an object, whatever it may be, which produces the emotion of sublimity.

What is wit? That which produces a peculiar effect when cognized, which effect we term the emotion of the ludicrous. We can no more tell in what wit consists, than we can tell in what truth consists. Attempts to reduce it to a single principle or characteristic have failed. A great variety of thoughts and relations are witty.

The lowest form of wit is termed humor, and may be possessed by one by no means remarkable for intellectual power. The higher forms of wit require a nice discrimination, which is allied to intellectual power. It has sometimes been said that wit and judgment never meet in the same person. The question is one to be determined by observation.

Wit and judgment—that is, the capacity for cognizing the relations of the ludicrous, and capacity for cognizing the relations necessary to come to sound conclusions—are not allied in the sense that the presence of the one indicates the presence of the other. A man may have a sound practical judgment, and be almost wholly incapable of cognizing ludicrous relations; but, on the other hand, I think it will be found that the person who has wit in its highest power—that is, power to cognize those relations which constitute the highest form of wit—will have power to cognize the relations necessary to the formation of sound opinions.

The fine arts, painting, poetry, music, sculpture, architecture, and gardening, have for their basis man's æsthetic nature—that is, his power of cognizing and enjoying beauty. They are said to be addressed to the eye and ear; but properly speaking, they are addressed to the mind. They should receive due attention from all who would give to their minds a full and harmonious development.

Beauty should be studied in subordination to truth and goodness. " The effect of the Beautiful upon the soul," says Professor Shedd, "when unmixed, uncounteracted, and exorbitant, is enervation. . . . When the æsthetical prevails over the intellectual and moral, the prime qualities, the depth, the originality, and the power die out of letters, and the mediocrity that ensues is but poorly concealed by the elegance and polish thrown over it. Even when there is much genius and much originality, an excess of Art, a too deep suffusion of beauty, a too fine flush of color, is often the cause of a radical defect."

In further proof of his views, he refers to " John Milton, one of those two minds which tower high above all others in the sphere of modern literature. If there ever was a man in whom the æsthetic was in complete subjection to the intellectual and moral, without being in the least suppressed or mutilated by them, that man was Milton. If there ever was a human intellect so entirely master of itself, of such a severe type, that all its processes seem to have been the pure issue of discipline and law, it was the intellect of Milton. In contemplating the grandeur of the products of his mind, we are apt to lose sight of the mind itself, and of his intellectual character. If we rightly consider it, the discipline to which he subjected himself, and the austere style of intellect and of art in which it resulted, are as worthy of the reverence and admiration of the scholar as the 'Paradise Lost.' We have unfortunately no minute and detailed account of his every-day life; but from all that we do know, and from all that we can infer from the lofty, colossal culture and character in which he comes down to us, it is safe to say that Milton must have subjected his intellect to a restraint, and rigid dealing with its luxurious tendencies, as strict as that to which Simeon Stylites or St. Francis of Assisi subjected their bodies. We can trace the process, the defecating, purifying process, that went on in his intellect, through his entire productions. The longer he lived, and the more he composed, the severer became his taste, and the more grandly and serenely beautiful became his works. It is true that the theory of art, and of culture, opposed to that which we are recommending, may complain of the occasional absence of beauty, and may charge as a fault an undue nakedness and austerity of form. But one thing is certain, and must be granted by the candid critic, that whenever the element of Beauty is found in Milton, it is found in absolute purity. That severe refining process, that test of light and fire, to which all his materials were subjected, left no residuum which was not perfectly pure. And therefore it is, that throughout universal literature, a more absolute Beauty, and a more delicate aërial grace, are not to be found than appear in the 'Comus,' and the Fourth Book of 'Paradise Lost.'"

CHAPTER XIX.

COGNITION OF RECTITUDE.

WE see a person inflicting a severe blow upon an unoffending stranger. We cognize by the eye the blow and its physical effects. We also cognize the fact that it was wrong. When we say that the blow was wrong, we mean that the person did wrong in giving the blow.

Will any one ask, How do we know that the blow was wrong? We know it, just as we know that the blow was struck. We saw the blow, and saw that it was wrong. In both cases it was the mind that saw. If we can trust the mind's cognitive power in regard to the blow, we can trust it in regard to the moral character of the blow.

We see a man in danger of drowning. Another rescues him. We see the act, and we also see that it is right.

We see one giving another money. We do not know whether the act is right or wrong. If it be in payment for goods purchased, it is right; if it be given in bribery, it is wrong. In this case, the cognition of the moral character of the act is not direct, as in the former cases. It is conditioned upon a cognition of the motive of the giver.

In simple and clear cases, the cognition of the moral character of an action is intuitive; in complex cases, the cognition is inferential—that is, is conditioned on preceding cognitions. Hence, in complex cases, there is liability to error: different minds may come to different conclusions as to the moral character of an act.

There is thus a difference between right and wrong. We know that there is a difference between right and wrong actions, just as we know that there is a difference between white and black objects: we cognize the fact in both cases. Nothing is gained by saying that reason makes known to us the distinction; for reason is not something distinct from us—our minds. We may ascribe some acts of the mind to reason and some to the understanding; but if the mind is one, those terms simply express different modes of its action. When the mind is cognizing contingent truth, it is said by some to be exercising the understanding; when it is cognizing necessary truth, it is said to be exercising the reason. The real distinction relates to the nature of the truth cognized.

Some seem to think that the mind does not arrive at truth in regard to morals in the same way in which it arrives at truths in regard to agriculture and politics. A special organ must be constructed and endowed with infallibility. Reason or conscience must be endowed with powers transcending other faculties, that it may make known to us the difference between right and wrong, and authoritatively tell us our duty. Numerous errors in regard to the elements of morality have resulted from this personification of reason and conscience.

It may be asked, " Has not man a conscience to make known to him his duty ? "

What is meant by the expression, " Man has a conscience" ? Simply that man has the power of cognizing right and wrong actions. The mind can cognize right and its opposite; man has a conscience; the mind possesses a moral faculty: all these are identical expressions.

It may be said, " All men do not agree in their views of right and wrong. If man is endowed with a moral faculty—if conscience is possessed by all men— then all men would have the same views as to moral questions. Sight is possessed by all men, and hence all men agree in distinguishing black from white. There are no instances in which some men contend that white is black; but there are frequent examples of men differing in regard to the same action—some regarding it as right and others as wrong."

The inference thus drawn is not legitimate. It does not follow from the premise, " All men are endowed with the power of cognizing the difference between right and wrong," that all men will agree in regard to the moral character of all actions. The inference as drawn by the objector is founded on the assumption, that if the mind has power to cognize the moral qualities of actions, it must be infallible in the exercise of that power. This assumption is unauthorized. The mind is not infallible in any of its mediate cognitions. Men have the power of distinguishing truth from falsehood. They know that the assertion, "The whole is greater than its part," is true, and that the assertion, "The whole is less than its part," is false. But the fact that the mind has thus power to cognize truth, does not prove that its cognitions of truth must in all case be infallible, and that all men will think alike on all questions relating to truth.

Some truths are simple and self-luminous. In regard to such truths all men agree in their cognitions. Some truths or questions are complicated, and can be cognized only through the medium of other truths. Hence there is liability to error. Hence there will be diversities of judgments. But diversities of opinion in regard to what is true and false in certain cases, do not prove that the mind has not the power to cognize truth — do not prove that there is no difference between truth and error. In like manner, diversities of opinion in regard to what is right and wrong in certain cases, do not prove that the mind has not power to cognize rectitude—do not prove that there is no difference between right and wrong.

Every one is conscious that he has power to cognize rectitude—that is, to cognize the moral quality of actions. How does he know that others have this power—that it is an attribute of humanity?

He infers from the actions of others that they have this power.

How does he know that men in other lands and in other ages possessed this power?

The proof of the fact is found in the structure of every language and in every historic record. In every language there are words expressive of right and wrong, of obligation, of praise and blame. Words are expressive of ideas: the people using those languages had ideas of right and wrong, of obligation, of praise and blame—that is, had the power of cognizing the moral quality of actions. Every code of laws that has come down to us, recognizes moral distinctions. There have been unjust laws; yet the statutes of all nations have a wonderful agreement in forbidding that which is wrong and allowing that which is right.

The approbation which the heroes of history have received, is based on the supposed possession of good qualities. Bad men have been honored, but not because they were bad.

Conscience, then, is an original attribute of our nature; in other words, all men have the power of cognizing the moral qualities of actions. The mind is not infallible in the exercise of this power. It may form erroneous conclusions in regard to duty, and it may form erroneous conclusions in regard to questions of political economy.

In regard to some actions, all men's cognitions are the same. In regard to some actions, the cognition of the moral quality is intuitive. All men's intuitions in regard to a given truth are the same. In other words, some truths are self-evident, and in regard to such truths all men agree. The axioms of geometry are self-evident, and all men agree that they are true. There are self-evident truths in morals. In regard to these all men agree.

That benevolence is right and malignity is wrong, are self-evident truths. In regard to such truths, the cognitions of all men are the same. It is not affirmed that all men would assent to the generalized statement that malignity is wrong; but let an act of wanton, unprovoked malignity be witnessed, and all men would see that it is wrong. Let an act of true benevolence be witnessed, and all men would approve it as right. Differences of opinion, as has been before remarked, may take place in complicated cases, where the steps taken to reach the conclusion are numerous, and depending upon truths which may be imperfectly apprehended. White and black are clearly distinguishable by all men when white and black objects are before them, and so of other colors. But let two colors be blended, as in the structure of the rainbow, and it is difficult to say where one color ends and the other begins. If men were required to state which color predominated at a particular point, there would be diversities of opinion, though there would be none as to the difference between the two colors. So the difference between right and wrong is clearly seen in simple cases. In complicated ones, there will be diversities of opinion.

In what does rectitude consist? What constitutes a right action? We have seen that we cannot answer similar questions asked with reference to truth. We cannot tell in what truth consists; we cannot tell what constitutes a true proposition. We are in the same condition in relation to these questions when asked with reference to rectitude. When, with respect to a particular act, it is asked, What constitutes its rightness? we may be able to give an answer. For example: I see one giving money to relieve a person in distress. The act is a right one. Why is it right? Because kindness to the distressed —benevolence—is right. On what does the rightness of benevolence depend? It may be said that it is right because God commands it. With reverence be it asked, on what does the rightness of God's command depend? A number of questions may be asked, but the point to which we shall be brought is a confession of our inability to state in what right consists.

It will be asked, Does not the rightness of an action consist in its tendency to promote happiness? The rightness of a particular action may be made known to us by its tendency to promote happiness; but the question may be asked, Why is it right to promote happiness?

The followers of Paley and Bentham affirm that the moral difference between actions is founded wholly on their tendency to promote happiness or misery. Those actions which tend to promote happiness are right, and right on that account alone; and those actions which tend to cause misery are wrong, and wrong on that account alone. The question, Why are actions tending to happiness right? remains unanswered.

We may admit that right actions tend to promote happiness; but it does not prove that their rightness consists in this tendency. In many cases, we intuitively cognize an act to be right before we take the consequences into view—when we are wholly ignorant of the consequences. The mind clearly distinguishes between utility and rightness. These are not identical. Let the appeal be made to consciousness.

If the theory under consideration were true, then if murder, malignity, and treason were followed by the greatest amount of happiness, they would be right. This conclusion, so diametrically opposed to our intuitive cognitions, is sufficient to show the unsoundness of the theory.

Again, on this theory a system of morals would be impossible to one of less than infinite knowledge.

Indeed, a finite mind could never settle a single question of duty. We wish to know whether an action is right. If there is no difference in actions except in relation to their consequences, then we wish to know whether the action will be followed by more happiness than misery during the whole duration of our being. Infinite knowledge would be required to determine whether the action is right or wrong; and infinite knowledge is not ours.

The tendency of an action to promote happiness no more constitutes its rightness, than the tendency of mathematical truths to utility constitutes their trueness. There are certain mathematical principles or truths useful to the engineer. Their tendency, if rightly applied, is to make his work secure. Their utility is a fact—a fact clearly distinguishable from their truth. Moral truths, rightly applied, are useful—render the structure of happiness stable; but their utility is clearly distinguishable from their rightness.

As it is conceded that we are under obligation to do right, if doing right consists in securing the greatest amount of happiness, then if we could secure more happiness by serving Satan than by serving God, we should be under obligation to do so!

Why are we under obligation to do right? Attempts have been made to answer this question—to give a reason for doing right—to prove that we ought to do right. The consequence has been, that obscurity has been thrown upon a subject naturally clear. This is always the consequence of attempts to prove self-evident truths.

Why should we believe a true proposition when it is clearly set before the mind? Because it is true. Why should we do right? Because it is right. The obligation to do right is involved in the perception of right; or it may be stated thus: It is a self-evident truth, that we are under obligation to do right. No truth clearer than this can be brought to prove it. We may state advantages following right doing, and disadvantages following wrong doing. But these facts only show that it is prudent to do right; they do not add to the force of the obligation.

It may be said that we should do right because God commands it. Undoubtedly all God's commands are right, and it is our duty to obey them. But the fact that it is right for us to obey God's commands, does not prove that God created the distinction between right and wrong—that things which are right are so simply because He commands us to do them. That which is created, is created in time—that is, at some time. Now, was there ever a time when malignity was right and benevolence wrong? Has God always been just and holy? Has He always been a hater of iniquity? Then the distinction between holiness and iniquity has always existed—there never was a time when it began to be.

The question, Why should we obey God's command? remains as yet unanswered. The true answer is, because it is right to do so. It may be said, we should obey Him because He is our Creator. Why does the creature owe obedience to its Creator? It will be said, because He made him. Suppose the maker of man were an unholy being, and commanded man to practise iniquity. Suppose man's moral nature to be as it now is, would it be right for man to practise iniquity? If it would not, then the mere relation of Creator and creature does not of itself involve the duty of obedience on the part of the latter. Suppose—with reverence be it spoken—that God's commands should be the opposite of what they are; suppose He should command us to be sinful, would it be right for us to be sinful? We know that it is impossible for Him to command that which is not right, just as it is impossible for Him to lie; but if it were possible, and were done, would not our obligation to obedience cease?

Will it be said, If God command me to murder a man, it would be right to do so? If God were to command you to take the life of a man, it would be right for you to do so. But to take the life of a man in obedience to God's commands, is one thing; and to take the life of a man with malice prepense and in violation of God's command, is another thing. The latter is murder, the former is not.

God could not authorize murder. His perfections

forbid it. He can authorize one to take the life of another. All souls are His, and He may dispose of them according to His righteous will. Whatever may be the case in regard to sinless beings, we have sinned, and forfeited our lives to His justice. He may therefore take our lives in any way that He chooses—by disease, or by the instrumentality of men.

While God cannot change wrong into right, yet, whenever He commands us to perform an act, it becomes moral, though before it was indifferent. In many cases it is a matter of indifference what kind of dress we wear; we may wear this or that, without doing wrong. If God were to command us to wear a particular dress, it would be wrong for us not to do so. So far as there are actions without a moral character, they become moral and obligatory when commanded by Him.

Men are under obligation to do what is right— not what they may think is right. It is a popular error, that sincerity in error changes the moral character of acts consequent upon that error. It is thought that if a man sincerely believes he is right, his action will be right.

Sincerity in error in physical matters does not affect the consequences of the error. If a man building a tower sincerely believes that he has so constructed it that the line of gravity falls within the base, and yet it falls without the base, his sincerity will not prevent the tower from falling. Sincerity in error will not reverse the law of gravitation.

If a man intending to visit a city lying eastward, by mistake takes a road leading northward, he may sincerely believe he is right, but he will not reach the desired city. Sincerity in error cannot change the point of compass. Can it change the supreme law of right, to which even God himself is subject?

A man may sincerely believe that he is doing God's will when he is going contrary to that will— as Paul thought he was doing God service when he was persecuting unto death the followers of Christ. It is true that failure to do God's will in such circumstances may be attended with less guilt than when the failure is the result of wilful passion; still, if one has acted contrary to God's will, he has done wrong. Thinking a thing to be right will not make it right, any more than thinking a thing to be true will make it true. It is singular that an error so transparent as that under consideration should have had so wide an influence.

Intention to do right is not doing right; it is a necessary condition of doing right. Intention to take the right road is not taking the right road; nor does it of necessity lead to taking the right road.

The right road may be taken by accident, but we can never do right by accident.

It is said that the moral character of an act lies in

the intention. Intention is the condition of performing a moral act, not the constituting quality of the act. Intention is used in two senses. Sometimes it means the motives prompting to action. Suppose the act to be the payment of a just debt. The act in itself is right; but if the debtor pay it solely through fear of an arrest, he does not do his duty—does not do right. Here it is seen that in order to perform a right action, the act must be in itself right, and it must be performed from right motives.

Intention is also used in the sense of volition. A man may conform to a physical law without intending to do it. A farmer, though ignorant of an important law of vegetation, may conform to it, and he will reap all the advantages resulting from conformity to that law. But a purpose to obey, a voluntary obedience to moral law, is essential; there can be no obedience in ignorance or by accident. We must know what the law is, and voluntarily conform to it.

Moral qualities belong to actions. Actions are performed by the intelligent, accountable mind. The body is the instrument of the mind. Bodily changes, physical acts as they are sometimes termed, considered apart from the mind, have no moral character. The motion of the limbs occasioned by the action of a galvanic battery has no moral character. The motion of the limbs as caused by the volitions of the mind has a moral character. The volitions are a part of the mental act; and the dispositions and desires leading to the volition are a part of the act, and come within the view of the mind, when it decides that the act is right or wrong.

In order to a perfect moral action, the act itself, that is, the end sought to be effected, must be right; the intention must be right, and the action of mind and body must correspond with the intention.

Some actions are intrinsically right—for example, acts of honesty and benevolence: some actions are intrinsically wrong, such as acts of malignity and treachery. Some actions are neither right nor wrong in themselves, but are right or wrong according to circumstances. It may not be wrong for me to sway my body backwards and forwards in my own study; but it would be wrong for me to do so in the house of God during public worship.

Is morality predicable of dispositions and habits as well as of voluntary actions? Some affirm that morality is predicable only of voluntary actions; but, in order to include all things plainly moral, they give an unauthorized extension to the term voluntary. They make it include our desires and affections. A man earnestly desires to exercise revenge upon another—earnestly desires to injure him. He puts forth no voluntary act designed to injure him, because he has no opportunity. The desire is clearly distinguishable from a volition—an act of the will— that is, of the mind willing. Is the desire destitute of a moral character? Is it not as clearly wrong as a volition causing a blow is wrong?

There may be thus virtuous and vicious desires. In like manner, there may be virtuous and vicious dispositions and habits.

Dispositions and habits are not acts, but conditions of mind causing acts, and determining their moral character. A man who is constantly performing benevolent acts, forms a habit of benevolence. A man who is continually performing selfish acts, forms a habit of selfishness. These habits form a portion of the character of each. Is the character of the one praiseworthy, and the character of the other blameworthy; or are our approbation and disapprobation confined to the voluntary actions?

I think the general sense of mankind attributes virtue and vice to dispositions and character as well as to strictly voluntary acts. It would be more correct to say that the moral character of our actions depends upon our dispositions, rather than that morality is confined to our volitions.

Men are under obligation to do right—to do right in all things and at all times. Have they power to do so? Is man's ability commensurate with his obligation?

In his present fallen condition, man is not able to act with perfect uprightness—to be perfectly holy. He is fallible in his judgments, and hence often fails to form right ideas as to his duty. We must know our duty perfectly in order to perform it perfectly. In order to perfect holiness, there must be a perfect knowledge of duty, and this man does not possess.

Does man's ignorance of duty excuse him from performing it? The answer depends upon the causes of his ignorance. If he is wilfully ignorant—ignorant because he will not use his powers aright—if he is misled by prejudice and passion, he is responsible for the causes of the ignorance, and consequently for the ignorance itself.

Suppose man has a perfect knowledge of duty: has he ability to perform it perfectly—to be perfectly holy?

Man was originally endowed with full power to do his whole duty—to be perfectly holy. But the Scriptures teach that by the fall and by his wilful transgressions his capacity for right doing has been lessened. It is conceded by all that a man, by forming sinful habits, diminishes his power to do right. He diminishes his power to see duty and to do it. Is his obligation to do right thereby lessened? or may the moral Governor hold him responsible for not doing all that he could have done, if he had not lessened his moral power?

Some think that, in this case, man is responsible only for what he has power to do—no matter how the lack of power was occasioned. They hold him punishable for the act of lessening his power, but not accountable for doing that which would have been his duty had he not lessened his power.

To this it may be objected, that it makes God's claims dependent upon the will of the sinner. Just so far as the sinner lessens his power to do right, God's claims to obedience are lowered. A new law must be made for the sinner every day; or rather, he makes a new law for himself!

If, in proportion as the sinner lessens by sinning his moral power, God's claims to his obedience are lessened, then if he could destroy all his power to do right, God would have no claims to his obedience at all. He would be a subject of punishment, but not subject to the law of holiness. Is it reasonable to suppose that a man by sinning can place himself without the domain of God's law? Is not God's law immutable and binding forever on every moral being?

We find that men are in fact unable to perfectly obey God's law; and yet God commands them to be holy as He is holy. It would seem, therefore, that God claims that which man, in his fallen condition, is unable to perform. We are here met by a difficulty that human wisdom cannot solve. Men are born without the requisite power to render perfect obedience to God's law: their power is lessened still more by voluntary transgression; but this is the result of a native tendency to evil. Whence this strange condition? The Bible informs us that it is the result of

Adam's sin. Whether one accept the explanation or not, the difficulty still remains.

The present disordered condition of the human mind, whether it be regarded as a consequence of Adam's sin, or whether it be regarded as the result of creation, is a mystery that the future may solve. At present it is one of those things in regard to which it may be said, " clouds and darkness are round about him." Still, this should never for a moment permit us to doubt the truth, that "justice and judgment are the habitation of his throne." We must not deny a well-established fact because we cannot give a satisfactory explanation of it.

The difficulty above noted is in nowise chargeable to revealed religion. Man is as he is, whether the Bible be a revelation from God or not. Revelation proposes a remedial system, and in its perfect adaptation to fallen man is found one of the strongest arguments for its truth.

Much is said about the duty of obeying the dictates of conscience: what is meant by the expression? Acting in accordance with our perceptions of right.

Do we always do right when we obey conscience? That is, do we always do right when we think we are doing right? Are our moral judgments always correct? Or does our thinking a thing to be right, make it right?

To ask, Ought we always to obey conscience? is to

ask, Ought we always to do what we think is right? The reply to this is obvious. We are not to act contrary to our convictions of duty; but then our views of duty should be accurate.

Suppose one fully believes it to be his duty to persecute those whom he regards as heretics. In popular language, his conscience tells him he ought to do it. If he obeys his conscience, if he acts according to his erroneous convictions of duty, he does wrong; for it is not God's will that any one should persecute others. If he disobeys his conscience, acts contrary to his erroneous conviction of duty, he does wrong. The wrong consists, it is said, in violating his conscience; but this simply means that he refused to act in accordance with his convictions of duty. The wrong consists in acting contrary to what he believed to be the will of God. He believed it to be God's will that he should persecute; but from tenderness of heart, or fear of public opinion, he declined to do what he believed to be God's will, and thus was guilty, in principle, of disobeying God—just as a child may be guilty of disobedience to his parent, by refusing to do what he believed his parent commanded, though that belief was erroneous.

We see thus that a man, by entertaining wrong opinions, may be in a condition in which he will do wrong whether he acts or refrains from acting. Is he then to blame?

That depends on the causes of his being in that

position. If the cause was his neglect to investigate and understand the truth on which his duty was conditioned, he is of course responsible for being in that unhappy position.

We are under obligation to have right views of duty, and to act in accordance with those views. Hence we see the importance of a knowledge of religious truth, so much insisted on in the Scriptures. An orthodox creed is an essential condition of an orthodox life.

Are we to decide questions of duty for ourselves, or are we to defer to the judgment and authority of others? Are we ever to act contrary to our convictions of right from regard to the authority of others?

We have seen that one is under obligation to know his duty—to know it himself. Whatever aid he can get from others in arriving at true conclusions in regard to duty, he is under obligation to get; but he cannot throw upon others the responsibility of deciding. He must act for himself, and therefore he must think for himself: thinking, in such cases, is not separable from action. Every one must give account of himself unto God. Priest or potentate cannot answer for him; therefore they are not to decide questions of duty for him.

It has been said by some men of great reputation, that in regard to religious matters a man's own conscience is to be his guide, but that in regard to civil matters the law of the land, and not conscience, is to be his guide.

To say that a man's conscience is to be his guide in religious matters, is to say that he is to decide for himself what his duty is in regard to religion, and to do it.

To say that the law, as distinguished from conscience, is to be one's guide in civil matters, is to say that one is to do what the law enjoins, whether he regards it as right, as according to the will of God, or not.

This view implies a distinction in regard to human actions which does not exist. It is not true that some of our actions are religious, and others civil or secular. God's will has respect to all our actions. Whether we eat or drink, or whatsoever we do, we are to do all to the glory of God—to do all with reference to pleasing God. Acts pertaining to government have a moral character, are religious acts, as truly as acts pertaining to the public worship of God. It is God's will that men should worship Him: it is also His will that they should obey magistrates. In all things God's will is to be our guide. This is what is meant when it is said conscience should be our guide.

Again, this view implies that rulers have the power of changing moral distinctions—if not of creating them. If the law is to be our guide, then whatever the law enjoins must be right. Suppose it enjoins idolatry—are we to worship idols? Can a legislature or a despot change the ten commandments? The apostles said, we ought to obey God rather than man.

The true doctrine is plain. Government is a divine institution. It is our duty to obey all the laws, unless they come in conflict with the law of God. Every one must decide for himself whether in a given case there is a conflict or not. If the law commands him to do what is wrong, or what he thinks is wrong, he is to refuse to obey, and submit to the penalty. If it inflicts wrong upon him at the hand of others, he is to suffer it without resistance; unless the oppression is so great as to justify a revolution—that is, a forcible overthrow of the oppressive government, and the establishing of another in its place. The fact that a law is unwise and unjust, does not authorize us to disobey it, or forcibly resist its execution. It is often our duty to suffer wrong. When the wrong is wellnigh intolerable, and there is a fair prospect that an attempt to overthrow the government and establish a better one would be successful, then a people are justified in resorting to the right of revolution.

Thus it may be our duty to submit to a government, for a time at least, which had its origin in injustice and cruelty. The fact that we are commanded to pay tribute to Cæsar, does not prove that Cæsar has a right to sway the sceptre of absolute authority, and that it would not be right to dethrone him if we had the power. The fact that a slave is commanded to obey his master, does not prove that the master has a right to his obedience. Rights and duties, when different persons are concerned, are not always reciprocal. It may be my duty to obey a highwayman till such time as I can put a bullet through him.

The view under consideration destroys the right of private judgment, and hence destroys personal accountability. Man is no longer responsible for his conduct in civil matters. His responsibility is thrown on the government. It may just as well be thrown on the priest or the pope.

This view was adopted in consequence of an illogical conclusion drawn from the proposition, that every man should follow his convictions of duty in civil as well as religious matters. The conclusion was, that every man would be at liberty to do that which was right in his own eyes—that anarchy would be the result. One man would think that one law was wrong, and would disobey it; and another, another: consequently, the authority of law would be at an end.

No such conclusion can be legitimately drawn from the premises. Every man is under obligation to act according to his convictions of duty; he is also under obligation to have his convictions of duty accurate. If his convictions are accurate, he will conscientiously obey all laws except those which are really in conflict with the law of God, and no one will contend that any government can nullify the law of God. Suppose his convictions of duty are inaccurate—that he thinks that a law is opposed to the law of God when it is not: he will not obey it; he will disobey, and suffer the penalty. He thus recognizes the authority of government. He makes no resistance to the laws. In fact, he renders a passive obedience to the law. Anarchy cannot take place where every law is either actively or passively obeyed—where every law is obeyed, or the penalty of non-obedience submitted to.

Can conscience be perverted? That is, can the mind come to wrong conclusions in respect to duty? Of course, as it is fallible, it may err in regard to questions of duty as in regard to all other questions. The error may result from an inaccurate view of the facts of the case, or from an obtuseness of perception.

The mind's power of cognizing duty may be impaired by neglecting to exercise it aright. The susceptibility of feeling may be in like manner decreased. Sin blinds the mind—lessens its discriminating power, and hardens the heart—renders the mind less susceptible of enjoyment or suffering, as duty is or is not performed.

Can conscience be eradicated—can the mind lose its power of cognizing moral distinctions, and its power of feeling remorse? We have seen that by wrong doing the discriminating and emotive power may be impaired: can it be annihilated? Can a man by sinning destroy his moral nature?

We have no reason to believe that such an event can take place. Conscience sometimes seems to slumber; that is, a man seems insensible to moral distinctions, and sins grievously without any apparent sense of guilt or remorse. But this slumber is often broken, and the mind seems to have all its discrimination and moral sensibility restored.

What is meant by the supremacy of conscience? Simply, that we ought always to do right. Two plans of action are proposed: one will be productive of great pecuniary benefit, but will involve a course of wrong doing; the other proposes that which is strictly right. Of the two, we should adopt the latter: we were made to do right, and it can never be right to do wrong. We may say that one plan is dictated by the understanding, and the other by conscience, and thus be led to speak of a conflict between understanding and conscience; but the conflict is between the plans, not between two imaginary entities termed faculties. Both plans were apprehended by the mind. The mind sees that one is right, and the other wrong.

To say that conscience should be carefully cultivated, is to say that we should take the utmost pains to learn what is right, and to do it; that we should seek first the kingdom of God and his righteousness.

CHAPTER XX.

REASONING.

No mental process is more important than that of reasoning. Hence a clear explanation of it is desirable.

To give an explanation or analysis of the process of reasoning, is to state what the mind does when it reasons. As all men frequently perform acts of reasoning, it ought not to be difficult to describe the acts thus performed.

Reasoning is an act of the mind—not the act of a supposed faculty distinct from the mind, or forming a constituent portion of the mind. In regard to no mental process has personification been carried to greater excess than in regard to the process of reasoning. Reason, or the reasoning faculty, has been endowed with nearly all the attributes of personality. It is said to inform the mind, to receive from the senses facts and draw inferences from them; it is said to fall into error, and to lead the mind astray. This unfortunate use of language has thrown needless obscurity over the subject of reasoning. In considering this subject, let the student forget, for the time being, the existence of faculties; let him ignore the existence of Reason, and Judgment, and Comparison, and the like personages, and confine his attention to successive mental acts which constitute the process of reasoning. He will not find it to be so obscure and complicated a matter as it is commonly supposed to be.

It is the mind which reasons, just as it is the mind that cognizes external objects and remembers. Reasoning is a cognizing act of the mind. We cognize by reasoning truths which were unknown to us before. Reasoning, then, is the mental process of cognizing unknown truths, by means of those that are known. We can attend to this process in a given instance, and state the successive steps.

We have seen that some of our cognitions are direct, immediate, intuitive. Such are our cognitions of the existence of material objects, and of the self-evident truths termed axioms. But all our cognitions are not direct, immediate, intuitive. Our knowledge of some truths is conditioned upon our previous knowledge of other truths; that is, we see some things to be true in consequence of having seen some other things to be true. This last method of seeing is reasoning. If we observe what the mind does—what its successive acts are when it sees a thing to be true because it has previously seen another thing to be true—we shall observe the process of reasoning.

We are not at liberty to assume that the process of reasoning is in all cases identical. The effect of so doing is a liability to warp our facts to suit the assumption. This assumption has sometimes been made by those attempting to give an analysis of the process of reasoning. The mind may have different modes of procedure in cognizing unknown truths by means of known truths. When we have observed the process in different circumstances, and in regard to a variety of truths, we may be prepared to affirm that the reasoning process is or is not identical in all cases.

Before proceeding to consider an example of reasoning, we would remind the student that all conditioned cognition is not reasoning. We have some direct, intuitive cognitions conditioned on a previous cognition. Thus, our cognition of space is conditioned on our cognition of body. Our cognition of power is conditioned upon our cognition of change in an object. We cannot be said to arrive at a knowledge of space and power by reasoning. They have the directness and universality characteristic of intuitions.

Again, the cognition of certain relations is conditioned on previous cognitions. We cognize the resemblance between two pillars. The cognition is conditioned upon the previous cognition of the pillars. Objects must be known before the relations between them can be known. Hence the cognition of certain relations, though conditioned on other cognitions, is not reasoning.

This direct cognition of relations is generally termed a judgment. Hence we hear of judgment and reasoning—of reasoning being made up of judgments. The naming of an act does not alter its nature, though it may cause confusion in relation to it. The direct perception of the relation of similarity, superiority, equality, may be called a judgment, but it is no part of the process of reasoning—that is, of the process peculiar to reasoning. The term judgment is used in two senses: one, to express the cognition consequent upon comparing two objects; the other, to express the decision which the mind comes to when it has considered the evidence favorable and adverse to a particular proposition. It would be well to confine the use of the word to the latter sense.

Let us now examine some instances of reasoning, and observe the successive mental acts. Reasoning, as we have seen, is the mental process of cognizing unknown truths by means of those that are known.

Suppose I am passing along the street, and see dilapidated walls and the charred remains of timber. I infer that a building has been destroyed by fire. The facts directly perceived are the crumbling walls and charred remains, and yet I know that there has been a fire there. Using common language, I may say, I see there has been a fire there; but through the agency of sense I see only the evidences of fire. The truth that there has been fire there, is not a sense-perception—is not a direct perception, but an inference. It is a knowledge, however, and may have as much certainty attached to it as attaches to a direct perception.

Suppose I had never witnessed the action of fire: could I, on seeing the ruins, infer that a building had been destroyed by fire? Suppose I had witnessed the action of fire, but had entirely forgotten its effect: could I make the above inference from the sight of the ruins? A condition of the inference, then, is recollected knowledge. I infer that the present ruin is the effect of fire, because I have previously known that such is the effect of fire. The whole process of cognizing the fact that a fire destroyed the building, may be stated thus: 1. A sense-perception of the ruins. 2. A recollection of the effects of fire previously known. 3. An inference from analogy—illustrating the principle that like causes produce like effects—that the present ruins were caused by fire. All that is peculiar to the process is inferring. This is conditioned on sense-perception and recollected knowledge.

It may be said that I know from experience that the building was destroyed by fire. My experience is not experience pertaining to the case in hand. I have seen other buildings destroyed by fire. I did not see this building destroyed. Strictly speaking, I have had no experience in the matter. I have had experience in similar cases. How can I, then, decide that fire destroyed this building, because fire destroyed other buildings? I answer, the mind does thus decide. We must accept the fact that the mind does thus cognize the existence of fire as the cause of the ruin in question, as we accept the fact that it cognizes the existence of material objects when presented to the senses. Where the analogy is perfect, the cognition is one of certainty.

It may be said that the mind, in making an analogical inference, proceeds upon the principle that like causes produce like effects. When it is said the mind proceeds upon a certain principle, the meaning is not very clear. If by the expression is meant that the procedure or act exemplifies a certain principle, the meaning is clear. But if it be meant that the conclusion is an inference from the general fact, the meaning is not true. One sees a tree fall. He sees that there was some cause for its falling. But the truth that the fall of the tree had a cause, is not an inference from the general truth that every change has a cause. The cognition was intuitive. The mind, on seeing the fall of the tree, and cognizing the fact that it must have had a cause, may be said to proceed upon the principle that every effect must have a cause; but the cognition is not an inference from, but an exemplification of that principle. In like manner, the inference in the case under consideration is an exemplification of the truth, that like causes produce like effects.

Take another example of reasoning. I hear an organ in an adjoining apartment. It may be said that I know the organ is there because I hear it. But all that I hear is a sound. That is the sum of my direct cognition. I remember that I have heard similar sounds, and that I had a direct cognition that they were caused by an organ. I infer that the sound now heard is caused by an organ. The mental process is similar to the one above described. There is first a direct cognition—*i. e.*, sense-perception—of sound; secondly, recollected cognitions of similar sounds and their causes; thirdly, an inference from analogy that the present sounds are caused by an organ. The inference exemplifies the truth, that like causes produce like effects. We have in the process an act of cognition, an act of memory, and an act differing from both, viz., an inference. Reasoning is thus inferring unknown truths from those that are known.

A man is standing on the bank of a river. He wishes to place his fish-hook at the bottom of the river. He attaches a piece of lead to it, with the certainty that it will sink to the bottom. That the lead will sink, is an inference from analogy. The mental process is the same as in the two cases above noticed.

We have thus considered three cases of inferring —cases in which the inferences had reference to the past, the present, and the future. In each case, the certainty of the inference is proportioned to the exactness of the resemblance to former cases.

A farmer surveys his fields with reference to distributing his crops. He concludes that a certain field will yield a good crop of corn, because he has found from experience that soils of that description have yielded a good crop. He has had no experience connected with that particular field. He has had experience of similar fields. His inference is an inference from analogy. It will be true in proportion as the field in question, and attendant circumstances, are similar to those of which he has had experience.

The merchant determines to import a certain article, because he believes there will be a demand for it, and that he can sell it at a profit. His experience has taught him that, on former occasions, when the circumstances of the country were similar to present circumstances, there was a demand for the article in question. He infers that the article will be again in demand. The inference is founded on present and recollected cognitions. The facts which are the object of his present cognitions—which constitute the circumstances of the country—may be numerous and complicated. Some of them may be cognized by him directly, and some may be received on testimony, and some may be inferred from other facts. He is therefore liable to error in regard to his facts—in regard to the grounds of his inference. He may err as to the degree of similarity between the present circumstances of the country and the circumstances when the demand existed. The analogy may be so small, that the inference may not be accurate. But the mental process is the same as in the cases above described.

The physician is called to visit a patient. He finds the patient has a certain disease. He prescribes a certain medicine, which he is confident will work a cure. He may be asked the ground of his confidence, and he answers, he is acting from experience. He knows from experience that the medicine will cure the disease.

Now, what he really knows is, that the medicine was effective in a similar case. With the present patient he has had no experience. He has found that, in other similar cases, the medicine effected a cure; he therefore infers that it will work a cure in the present case. His judgments from experience are inferences from analogy, and will be sound in proportion to the strictness of the analogy between the condition of his present and former patients.

The statesman is said to be governed by experience—his individual experience, and the recorded experience of the past. He adopts such measures as experience has shown to be wise. He has learned that certain measures in certain circumstances have proved beneficial; he therefore concludes that similar measures in similar circumstances will prove beneficial. His conclusions from experience are inferences from analogy. Thus we have the type of all reasoning from experience. Reasoning from experience is inferring from analogy.

Let us next consider the ordinary argument for the existence of an intelligent First Cause of the world. We observe in nature indications of design. Design implies an intelligent designer. Hence the world had an intelligent Creator. We cognize certain facts. We know from experience what indications of design are. We have seen certain things which we know to be the work of design; hence, when we see analogous things in nature, we infer that they were the result of design. In the same way we know that design is the work of an intelligent cause, a person. The argument for the existence of God is thus an argument from analogy.

It thus appears that analogical reasoning comprehends a very large portion of our reasonings. It is not, as has been sometimes stated in books, a secondary and imperfect mode of reasoning, chiefly useful in answering objections. Nearly all the reasonings pertaining to practical life are reasonings from analogy. It is the type of by far the greatest portion of the reasonings of life.

The conclusions arrived at by analogy vary from

certainty to the lowest degree of probability. If you see footprints on the sand, you are perfectly sure that some person has been there. If you cast lead into the water, you are perfectly sure that it will sink. You meet with a stranger: you are perfectly sure that he is not infallible in all his conclusions. The certainty, in these cases, is the result of analogical inference.

You meet a large assemblage of uncultivated people, and find that they are partaking freely of intoxicating drinks. You infer that it is highly probable that there will be some disorder.

There is liability to error in reasoning from analogy. The error commonly is caused by an imperfect cognition of facts. An analogy is supposed to exist when it does not, or the analogy is less perfect than is supposed. False and imperfect analogies have been most fruitful sources of error.

The mind should be carefully trained to an accurate perception of analogies. It is a most important part of the training of a reasoner. One of the ablest lawyers of our country remarked to the author, "A perfect perception of analogies would make a perfect lawyer."

We do not reason by inferring: inferring is reasoning. Are analogical inferences the only inferences drawn by the mind?

Let it be proposed to prove the following proposition: The President did not affix his signature at

Washington to a certain document on the fourth of January. Let the truth be substantiated that the President was on that day, and during the whole of that day, at Boston. Of course, he could not affix his signature to a document in Washington. The inference is irresistible: on what is it grounded? On two facts or knowledges: the one, that a man cannot act where he is not; and the other, that the President was in Boston. If we were destitute of either of these knowledges, the inference would not be sound. We know from experience that a man cannot act where he is not, and from personal observation or testimony that the President was in Boston. The inference from these facts cannot fairly be classed under the head of analogy. In the case of a piece of lead being cast into water, the inference is from analogy. We have seen other pieces sink, and confidently believe that this will sink. Our belief is so strong, that we say we know it will sink.

When we know the facts above stated, we see that the signature was impossible. The inference is not a belief, however confident. It is a knowledge. We not only see that the proposition may be true: we see that it must be true. The process is clearly distinguishable from the analogical process. The principle illustrated in the analogical process is, like causes produce like effects. The principle or general fact illustrated in the case before us is, that a man cannot act where he is not. The inference may be called an inference from implication.

Take another example. One enters a portrait gallery. He sees a portrait which is a striking likeness of his friend B. On inquiry, he learns that it is the portrait of Mr. C. C is unknown to him, but he infers that he resembles his friend B. Here is an inference grounded on the fact that the portrait is a striking likeness of two different persons. In that fact is implied the fact that the two persons resemble each other. The inference is one of implication, and not of analogy. It may perhaps be stated in an analogical form, but the statement would be a forced one, and the principle illustrated is not the analogical principle. The general fact illustrated is, that things that resemble the same things resemble one another.

A man lost all his money yesterday; therefore he cannot pay a debt due. Here is a fact and an inference. The conclusion is implied in the fact.

Analogy is not, therefore, the type of all reasoning. We cognize some new truths by analogy, and others because implied in truths already known. The author has not examined any example of reasoning that does not come under the head of analogy or implication.

In reasoning from analogy, the process and the principle illustrated are always the same. In reasoning from implication, the process varies, or rather the principle illustrated differs as the facts or premises differ. This we should expect. The process consists in seeing a truth in consequence of its relation to another truth. Truths are connected by various relations. Hence, one truth introduces another to the mind's view by a relation different from that by which another truth introduces one. In other words, we should not expect to find all truths implied in other truths in the same way.

CHAPTER XXI.

MATHEMATICAL REASONING.

MATHEMATICAL reasoning is reasoning concerning mathematical truth. It is cognizing unknown mathematical truths by means of those that are known. Certainty attaches to mathematical reasoning, but this does not constitute the difference between mathematical and moral reasoning; that is, reasoning on subjects that are mathematical and those that are not mathematical—reasoning relating to necessary truth and to contingent truth. Some of our conclusions from contingent truths are as certain as are all our conclusions from necessary truths. The conclusions in some of the examples above given are as certain as any of the conclusions of geometry; and to affirm the opposite is as absurd as to affirm the opposite of the conclusions of geometry. To affirm that a man in Boston can write his sign manual in Washington, is not less absurd than to say that two lines that are equal to a third line are not equal to one another.

It has been said that the certainty of geometrical

reasoning is owing to the exactness of its definitions, and that a similar exactness in our definitions in morals and politics would secure a similar certainty in moral and political reasoning. The remark is founded on a misapprehension as to the nature of the definitions of geometry. They are not arbitrary constructions depending upon the skill of the writers on geometry. They are not creations of the mind. They are statements of necessary truths. They are statements of facts respecting space and its relations. A straight line is a certain relation in space between two objects or points in space. Angles are certain combinations of straight lines. So of other geometrical figures described in the definitions. The definitions are statements of facts in relation to space, as the definitions of geology are statements of facts in regard to the earth.

They are not mere conceptions of the mind—hypotheses, from which we infer hypothetical truth. They are realities—that is, real truths in relation to space, which are cognized as soon as they are set before the mind.

If they were mere hypotheses, mental figments, we should be at liberty to vary them; but this has not been done, and cannot be done. Writers on geometry have differed slightly in their modes of expression when stating the definitions; but all have directed the mind to the same truths. If they are hypotheses, they are mere creations of the mind.

The uniform agreement of geometers in regard to them is inexplicable on the supposition that they are hypotheses, but perfectly explicable on the supposition that they are cognized relations of space—necessary truths.

It is objected to this view, that had we never seen a material line, angle, or circle, we could not understand the definitions of geometry. Doubtless our first ideas of lines, angles, and circles, are received through the agency of the senses. Our primary cognitions are probably cognitions by the senses. Our cognition of space is conditioned on our cognition of matter. In like manner, our cognition of the relations of space—forms of shape, may be conditioned on our cognition of material forms.

Mill denies that the definitions of geometry have any existence—denies that there are any geometrical forms distinct from material forms. He says: "There exist no points without magnitude, no lines without breadth, nor perfectly straight; no circles with all their radii exactly equal, nor squares with all their angles perfectly right. It will perhaps be said that the assumption does not extend to the actual, but only to the possible existence of such things. I answer that, according to any test that we have of possibility, they are not even possible. Their existence, so far as we can form any judgment, would seem to be inconsistent with the physical constitution of our planet, at least, if not of the universe. To get rid of this difficulty, and at the same time to save the credit of the supposed systems of necessary truths, it is customary to say that the points, lines, circles, and squares which are the subject of geometry, exist in our conceptions merely, and are part of our minds; which minds, by working on their own materials, construct an *à priori* science, the evidence of which is purely mental, and has nothing whatever to do with outward experience. By howsoever high authorities this doctrine may have been sanctioned, it appears to me psychologically incorrect. The points, lines, circles, and squares which any one has in his mind, are, I apprehend, simply copies of the points, lines, circles, and squares which he has known by experience. A line as defined by geometers is wholly inconceivable. We can reason about a line as if it had no breadth; because we have a power, which is the foundation of the control we can exercise over the operations of our minds; the power, when a perception is present to our senses, or a conception to our intellects, of *attending* to a part only of that perception or conception, instead of the whole. But we cannot conceive of a line without breadth; we can form no mental picture of such a line: all the lines which we have in our minds are lines possessing breadth. If any one doubts this, we may refer him to his own experience. I much question if any one who fancies that he can conceive what is called a mathematical line, thinks so from the evidence of his consciousness. I suspect it is rather because he supposes that unless such a conception were possible, mathematics could not exist as a science; a supposition which there will be no difficulty in showing to be entirely groundless.

"Since, then, neither in nature nor in the human mind do there exist any objects exactly corresponding to the definitions of geometry, while yet that science cannot be supposed to be conversant about nonentities; nothing remains but to consider geometry as conversant with such lines, angles, and figures as really exist; and the definitions, as they are called, must be regarded as some of our first and most obvious generalizations concerning those natural objects."

We admit that "there exist no real [*material*] things exactly conformable to the definitions;" but unless material things are admitted to comprehend all things, his assertion is not necessarily correct. We affirm that there exist real things exactly conformable to the definitions; that there are real relations of space, which are intuitively cognized when the mind's attention is directed to them.

He says, "We cannot conceive of a line without breadth," by which we suppose he means, we can form no mental picture of such a line. Material objects are the only objects of which we can form mental pictures. We can form no mental picture of the human mind, yet it is a reality. All spiritual truths are unpicturable. If reality were confined to the picturable, materialism would be the only true philosophy.

The definitions of geometry are then neither arbitrary creations of the mind, nor mere copies of material objects. If the former were true, the science of geometry would be wholly subjective. If the latter, then it would follow, as Mill affirms, that the peculiar certainty always ascribed to it "is an illusion."

Dugald Stewart taught that reasoning in geometry is built wholly upon the definitions. The definitions he regarded as hypotheses, and hence the results of demonstration as only hypothetically true.

We have seen that the definitions of geometry are statements of facts. Let us next consider the axioms. The axioms are generalized statements of self-evident truths. Like all intuitive truths, they are cognized by all men—are admitted by all. This has been denied. It has been said that the savages of the western world never cognized the axioms, and hence the assertion that all men cognize them is not true. It is true that the axioms of geometry, as they are stated in books, have not been present to the minds of all men. But it must be remembered, that truth of every kind is first cognized in particular or individual instances. Did the savage ever fail to perceive that the whole of a deer was greater than its part? Did he ever proceed to a division of the results of hunting on the opposite principle?

When an individual case occurred, did he ever fail to perceive that two arrows, each equal in length to a third, were equal to one another? The truths of which the axioms are the generalized statement are intuitively cognized by all men as instances occur. They are intuitive, necessary truths.

Mill affirms that the axioms "are experimental truths—generalizations from observation." Observe that a generalization from observation is one thing— a generalized statement of an intuitive cognition another thing. That all men are mortal, is a generalization from observation. A series of observations—that is, a number of observed facts—is necessary to a generalization. A single intuitive cognition renders the truth of the axioms as certain as a thousand cognitions. When we have seen two rods each equal to a third, we intuitively cognize their equality with each other; and the statement of the fact thus cognized in a general form constitutes an axiom. A single cognition gives us the axiom. We see that it is true and must be true from one example as well as from a thousand.

The question, Does geometrical reasoning depend upon the axioms or the definitions? has been earnestly discussed. Locke and others contended that the axioms contribute nothing to the reasoning. Stewart adopted the same view, and contended that geometrical reasoning depends upon the definitions. Whewell, whose view of the nature of the definitions approaches very nearly to the true view, contends that the axioms, as well as the definitions, must be admitted as first principles of geometrical reasoning.

The expression, first principles of reasoning, is equivocal. First principles may mean the facts from which the reasoning starts, or they may mean principles or truths from which all the truths of geometry are deduced. Thus it is sometimes said, that from a few simple truths the far-reaching science of geometry has been built up. The impression on some minds seems to be, that the science is constructed out of the few truths expressed in the axioms or definitions, or both, either by combination or deduction. It is, perhaps, a common impression, that the truths of every science are deduced from self-evident truths. This impression is in consequence of the fact, that when we trace our knowledge in any department of science to its origin, we arrive at self-evident truths. But it does not follow from this, that all our knowledge is deduced from those self-evident truths. Truth is deduced only from comprehensive truths, and self-evident truths are always simple. Self-evident truths may constitute the origin, but not the source of all our knowledge. It does not follow, because a knowledge of certain truths is necessary to the knowledge of other truths, that the latter are contained in the former. A truth may be the condition of my cognizing another truth, without containing that truth. So far is it from being true that the science of geometry is deduced from the axioms, it may be affirmed that no truth can be deduced from an axiom. Take any one of the acknowledged axioms (for some propositions which appear among the axioms in some treatises are really definitions), and try to deduce a truth from it. Take the axiom, "Things equal to the same things are equal to one another," and what truth can you deduce from it? None. It will be said, we prove propositions by its aid. Let that assertion be made good by an appeal to facts. Take the first problem of Euclid—to construct an equilateral triangle. The process of proving that the triangle constructed is equilateral, consists in showing that two sides of the triangle, viz., A and B, are equal, because radii of the same circle; and that the sides B and C are equal, because radii of the same circle. The sides A and C have thus been shown to be equal to B, therefore they are equal to one another. If the question be asked, On what ground is the conclusion made that A and C are equal? the reply may be, Because things equal to the same are equal to one another. The conclusion is supposed to be drawn from the axiom as a premise. But suppose one had never heard the axiom stated. He would perceive the equality of the two lines as soon as he had perceived their equality to a third line. In fact, the truth is seen before the axiom is quoted, and before it is called to mind. Of course, it cannot be drawn from the axiom. If we consult what takes place in our minds, we shall discover that, as soon as we see that A and C are equal to B, we see that they are equal to one another. We see that they are equal because they are equal; just as we see the tree before us, because it is before us.

In the demonstration, the conditions of the cognition of the equality of A to B and C to B are given, and then the truth of their equality to each other is announced. The question is asked, Why? and the reply is, "Because things equal to the same are equal to one another." A generalized statement of what is intuitively perceived to be true in a given case, is given as the reason of it; that is, the repetition of a truth is given as the reason of that truth! There is no reasoning in such a course of procedure.

Take another example. In the course of a demonstration, it is seen and stated that an angle A is a part of an angle B, therefore B is greater than A. It is not necessary to quote or to call to mind the axiom, The whole is greater than its part, before we cognize the fact that B is greater than A. It is intuitively perceived; and when we quote the axiom, our cognition is not affected by it. It is a mere repetition in a general form of the truth intuitively perceived in the case in hand.

It thus appears that conclusions in geometry are not deduced from the axioms—that the axioms have no probative force. If treatises on geometry were to omit all reference to axioms, the reasoning would be just as intelligible and irresistible as it is now.

It may perhaps be said, that if the axioms were not true, the steps in the demonstration which exemplify them would not be true. A little reflection will show that this is tantamount to saying, that if certain things were not true, they would not be true.

The truths of geometry are, then, not deduced from the axioms. Geometrical reasoning does not depend upon the axioms. The science of geometry is not built up of axioms.

Does geometrical reasoning, then, depend upon the definitions? In a certain sense it does. Geometrical reasoning depends upon the definitions in the same sense in which geological reasoning depends upon the rocks which constitute the facts of the science. The definitions are the facts which the geometer reasons about. He compares them, and cognizes relations existing between them. The new truths arrived at are not inferences, but intuitive cognitions. A demonstration is a series of intuitive cognitions conditioned upon preceding cognitions. At the outset the intuitive cognitions are conditioned on the truths contained in the definitions: each new cognition may be the condition of a new cognition, as each step in the ascent of a mountain may be the condition of a wider prospect.

A geometrical demonstration is a series of intuitive cognitions conditioned on preceding truths—starting with the truth contained in the definitions. The process is plainly distinguishable from that of inferring.

If the definitions are not truths, if they are mere mental figments, then the relations between them are figments, and that which is regarded as the most certain of all knowledge becomes unreal, fictitious. But the definitions are truths, self-evident, necessary truths. They are assented to by all as soon as clearly stated; that is, it is seen that space has, and must have, the relations indicated by the definitions. The certainty of the reasoning depends upon the nature of the truth reasoned about, and not upon skilfulness of definition. It is therefore unreasonable to demand mathematical demonstration in relation to contingent truths. No fact, that is, no contingent event, can be mathematically demonstrated.

It was stated above that a demonstration consists of a series of intuitive cognitions, each conditioned on preceding cognitions. Testimony and inference have no place in a demonstration; for every step must not only be seen to be true, but necessarily true, and the opposite impossible. The opposite of the truest testimony is often not impossible. The opposite of the soundest inference is not impossible. The truth of the above assertion in regard to geometrical demonstration can be tested by an analysis of a demonstration.

CHAPTER XXII.

THE SYLLOGISM.

It has been affirmed that the syllogism is *the* mode of reasoning in regard both to contingent and necessary truth. A syllogism consists of a major and minor premise and a conclusion. The following is an example:

All men are mortal:
Socrates is a man;
Therefore, Socrates is mortal.

It is affirmed that the reasoning process is the same in all cases. Whately says that "one of the chief impediments in attaining a just view of the nature and object of Logic, is the not fully understanding or not sufficiently keeping in mind the SAMENESS of the reasoning process in all cases." The syllogism he regards as the type of all reasoning, and the principle on which syllogisms are constructed "is the universal principle of reasoning." This universal principle is the Dictum of Aristotle, viz., "that whatever is predicated (*i. e.*, affirmed or denied) universally of any class of things, may be predicated in like manner (viz., affirmed or denied) of any thing comprehended in that class."

. "Now to *remind* one, on each occasion, that so and so is referable to such and such a class, and that the class which happens to be before us comprehends such and such things—this is *precisely all that is ever accomplished by reasoning.*"

If this is all, reasoning has a much less extended scope than is generally supposed. If the analysis we have given of contingent and demonstrative reason be true, the process is not in all cases the same; and the Dictum is not the universal principle of reasoning. The process by which we cognize truths previously unknown, is something more than a reminding that the object we are reasoning about belongs to a certain class of objects.

The following remarks of Bailey are worthy of attention: "The *Dictum de omni et nullo,* viz., that 'whatever is predicated universally of any class of things, may be predicated in like manner of any thing comprehended in that class,' is not only stated by logicians to be a general maxim, of the application of which every direct syllogism is a particular instance, but proclaimed to be the universal principle of reasoning.

"If we closely scrutinize the meaning of this maxim, undazzled by the somewhat magnificent and imposing phraseology in which it has been spoken of, we shall find it an obviously simple and undeniable proposition, viz., whatever is asserted of a class may be asserted of any species or individual of that class. A class, however, we must bear in mind, is not a collective or corporate whole, which, as a whole, possesses properties or attributes different from those of the individuals composing it; but what is predicated of it is predicated of every separate individual ranked under it. The proposition, 'All men are fallible,' affirms that every individual man is fallible; while the proposition, 'The army is large,' affirms of the body collectively something which it does not affirm of any single individual in it. If a class were such a collective body, the Aristotelian maxim could not be true.

"The dictum, therefore, it is plain, means neither more nor less than that whatever is predicated of every individual of a class, may be predicated of any individual, or any number of individuals, of that class. As, however, what can be truly predicated of any thing must be a property or attribute actually possessed, we may, if we choose, leave out predication altogether, and then the maxim will appear in a still simpler shape, as follows: What belongs to every individual of a class must belong to any individual of that class. However it may be expressed, it is obviously a self-evident and indisputable truth, like the other maxims we have just been considering; and this view of its coördinate character is sufficient of itself to determine the accuracy of the maxim which proclaims it the universal principle of reasoning.

10

"If this doctrine were true, every act of reasoning would be an exemplification of this one maxim, and might be ranged under it. In other words, all reasoning without exception would consist in concluding that an attribute belongs to some individual class, because it belongs to every individual of that class. No other reason, according to this theory, can possibly exist or be assigned. The sole ground on which we can argue that an individual thing possesses any attribute, is, that the thing belongs to a class, all the members of which possess the attribute."

From the examples of reasoning which have been given, the student can decide whether they all come under the head of what may be termed class-reasoning; whether the conclusion, be it an inference from analogy, or a cognition conditioned on preceding cognitions, is reached by referring the subject to a particular class or not.

The doctrine above stated assumes that all our reasonings proceed from general principles, which assumption is unauthorized and is contrary to fact. All reasoning at the outset proceeds from facts directly cognized. By reasoning from facts we acquire general conclusions, and may use these conclusions as premises or facts for further reasoning.

When we thus use a general conclusion as a premise, the whole reasoning rests upon the facts from which the conclusion was deduced.

General principles may be revealed to us, and we

may draw inferences from them. The absolute perfection of God is revealed to us: we may infer from it that such and such things cannot be done by him. If all our reasonings proceeded upon general principles—that is, if a general principle must in all cases form the major premise—then, in order that our reasoning be sound, the major premise must be revealed to us, or we must intuitively cognize its truth. But all our intuitions are of individual truths, not of general principles; and all general principles are not revealed to us. They are arrived at by induction, which is inferring from analogy.

That every argument may be stated in a syllogistic form, does not prove that the mind used the syllogistic form, in making the inference. The different steps in a geometrical demonstration can be stated in a syllogistic form; but the mind does not use that form in reaching the conclusion. In the problem above adduced, in which the object is to prove that the triangle constructed is equilateral, two sides are shown each to be equal to the third side, and consequently they are equal to one another. The mind sees their equality to one another as soon as it sees their equality to the third side. The argument may be stated in a syllogistic form.

Things equal to the same are equal to one another:
A and C are each equal to B;
Therefore, they are equal to one another.

We have seen that the conclusion follows as soon

as we see that A and C are equal to B. It is not drawn from the axiom. The axiom is merely the generalized statement of what is intuitively cognized in an invividual case. The mind made no use of the major premise in coming to the conclusion; the conclusion would have been reached just as quickly, if the major premise had never been heard of. Every step in a geometrical demonstration can be stated in the form of a syllogism. The remarks respecting the problem above noticed will apply to every geometrical syllogism.

Instead of all reasoning being resolvable into the syllogism, a large portion of syllogistic reasoning is resolvable into reasoning from analogy. Take the example given above :

All men are mortal:
Socrates is a man ;
Therefore, Socrates is mortal.

Here the thing to be proved, the unknown truth to be reached by means of the known, is the mortality of Socrates. What is it inferred from? According to the syllogism, from the major premise, "All men are mortal." But how does the reasoner know that all men, including Socrates, are mortal? For as Socrates is a man, his being mortal must be known, that the premise may be valid; that is, the thing to be proved must be known, in order that it may be proved!

It has been charged against the syllogism, that in the major premise it assumes the point to be proved;

that every syllogism is a *petitio principii*. The charge is good against the syllogism of which the above is the type.

The mortality of Socrates, or of any other man, is provable. What is the process of proof? All men who have lived heretofore have died: Socrates is like them—has the same attributes; therefore, Socrates will die. In other words, a great many beings like Socrates have died; therefore, he will die. The inference is plainly an inference from analogy. The real argument cannot be stated in a syllogism constructed in accordance with the dictum.

Men learn to reason by reasoning, and not by the study of treatises on logic, which are not necessarily logical treatises. The author has questioned quite a number of men eminent for power in reasoning, and in no instance was the study of a technical logic referred to as a source of that power. They learned to reason by reasoning.

In fact, logic as taught in the schools does not profess to teach one how to reason. It professes to teach him how to cast an argument into a syllogistic form, in order that its soundness or unsoundness may appear from the form of the syllogism, though the argument were not understood. It would furnish, as it were, a mechanical test of arguments.

May there not be a more excellent way—that of training the mind to look directly at the proposition in question, to scan the premises to see if they are true, and the inference to see if it be legitimate? If reasoning consists in perceiving certain relations existing between truths, the power of cognizing relations should be exercised in preference to the practice of formal rules. We learn to reason by reasoning, just as we learn to remember by remembering. Let the student select the best specimens of reasoning to be found in the language. Let him make those specimens the subject of a careful study. Let him note how such men as Marshall and Webster and other great reasoners reasoned, and let him go and do likewise.

The study of mathematics may form habits favorable to moral reasoning, but cannot make a moral reasoner; that is, cannot make one skilful in reasoning on subjects that are not mathematical. The exclusive devotion of the mind for a long time to mathematical reasoning, has a tendency to unfit one for moral reasoning. The mind forms the habit of demanding certainty at every step, and acquires no skill in weighing probabilities, and evolving the truth from conflicting evidences. To estimate probabilities, and to reconcile apparent contradictions, and to detect tendencies, are processes which the reasoner on practical matters has occasion to perform daily; and he who acquires skill in these processes is better fitted for practical life than he who has skill in the use of the calculus.

CHAPTER XXIII.

MEMORY.

OUR cognitions, feelings, and volitions are constantly changing. As they pass from consciousness, they leave the mind in a condition which renders their resuscitation possible. The mind can remember or recall its past operations.

How the mind remembers we cannot tell; that is, we cannot describe the act of remembering. We have seen that we cannot describe the act of perception; we can only state its conditions. We can pursue a similar course in regard to memory.

In order that a thing may be remembered, it must receive some degree of attention. Objects which receive little or no attention, are seldom remembered. That memory is conditioned on attention, is known to all.

The attention may be spontaneous or voluntary. The object of thought may be in itself so interesting, that the attention shall be spontaneously fixed upon it. In reading an interesting narrative, we may be conscious of no effort at attention, and yet the attention may be so intensely fixed upon it, that we may become insensible to objects around us. Such narratives are easily remembered. Hence, if we would have others remember what we say, we must make our discourse interesting.

The attention may, by an effort, an act of will, be fixed on objects which are not interesting—which do not attract spontaneous attention. To be able thus to fix the attention, is the chief characteristic of a well-disciplined mind. The habit can be gained only by repeated and long-continued effort.

Clear and definite apprehension is necessary to distinct remembrance. The idea cannot appear in memory with greater distinctness than it appeared in perception. Hence, he who is cultivating the power of clear seeing, is cultivating his memory also. The right culture of one power of the mind tends to the improvement of the other powers.

Objects which awaken emotion are more easily remembered than those which do not. The effect of the emotion may be to concentrate the attention upon the object. It is said that such objects make a deeper impression upon the mind, and are therefore the more perfectly remembered. The phrase is simply a repetition of the fact which it seeks to account for.

Repetition is favorable to remembrance. A story heard several times is remembered with all its details; if it is heard but once, only the outline is remembered. The more frequently an object is present to the mind, the more readily it is recalled.

Relying upon the mind's power to remember—or trusting to memory—is another condition of remembrance. This is the same thing as exercising the mind vigorously in remembering. The mind's power in regard to every kind of action is increased in proportion to the legitimate, vigorous exercise which it receives. Two persons may resolve to commit the same poem to memory. One, under a mistaken view of the relation of repetition to remembrance, reads it over a score of times before he attempts to repeat it. The other undertakes to repeat it after a single perusal, and refers to the book only when, after long-continued effort, he fails to remember the stanza at fault. The latter pursues the course best adapted to strengthen his memory.

The use of written memoranda is unfavorable to good habits of remembering. He who relies upon his memoranda, will not rely upon his memory. Power in remembering is thereby impaired. Self-reliance is as important in regard to memory as it is in regard to moral perception and voluntary action. One's memory will serve him just in proportion as he really trusts it. One of the ablest and most extensive practitioners of law in New York city never keeps a memorandum of the cases on hand. It is not known that he ever failed to attend to a case at the appointed time.

An orderly and natural arrangement of our knowledge is favorable to memory. A well-arranged discourse or essay, in which the thoughts are placed in their natural relations to each other, is easily remembered. Of a desultory, disconnected essay or discourse, we can remember only here and there a thought. This is owing to the fact that our thoughts succeed each other according to certain relations, or laws of association. Why they succeed each other according to these laws, we cannot tell.

Susceptibility, retentiveness, and readiness have been named as the qualities of a good memory; in other words, it is desirable that the mind should be able to commit to memory easily, retain that which is thus committed, and readily reproduce it when wanted. Some minds commit to memory rapidly, and quickly forget what they have committed. Some commit with difficulty, but retain it long. Some retain with fidelity, but recall it slowly. Commonly, slowness of recollection is not owing to any peculiar mental action in remembering. There is a great difference in minds with respect to rapidity and slowness of action. A mind whose general operations are slow, will be slow in remembering. Some minds are rapid, retentive, and ready with respect to remembering.

Some acts of memory are spontaneous, and some are voluntary; that is, voluntary efforts are necessary in order to recall the desired thought. Memory is not directly subject to the will. The mind cannot will the presence of any thought: the attempt presupposes the presence of the thought. We wish to remember something—we cannot tell what it is, for that would be to remember it. It seems to be utterly gone from our minds; and yet, if another thought is suggested, we can see at once that it is not the thought whose presence we desire. We make an effort to remember. The effort consists in fixing our attention on objects known to be connected with the forgotten thought—in putting the mind in a waiting attitude. By-and-by the thought is resuscitated: perhaps we can trace the successive associated thoughts which brought it to mind—perhaps not. Sometimes a thought seems to flash upon our minds without any apparent connection with any other thought. Are there such disconnected mental acts?

Dugald Stewart thinks the thoughts constituting the links in the chain of association pass so quickly that we do not remember their presence. Hamilton's explanation is based on his theory of latent, unconscious mental modifications.

Minds differ as to their power of remembering. This may be owing, in some cases, to original differences in the structure of the minds thus differing, and in some cases to culture. There is in the case of nearly all persons a necessity for the exercise of memory which produces a considerable degree of development.

Some men have an extraordinary capacity for

remembering dates and names, and an ordinary, perhaps inferior capacity of remembering ordinary things. "Others remember permanently, and without effort, localities, the faces of persons, and every form of external nature. Some have great facility in recollecting words and their relations to each other."

"That these differences," says Dr. Wayland, "can be accounted for in some degree by education, I have no doubt. In the most remarkable instances, however, they seem to depend chiefly upon natural endowment. I have known several persons who have been gifted with some of these forms of recollection in a very uncommon degree, and they have uniformly told me that the things which they remembered cost them no more pains than those which they forgot. All the account which they could give of the matter was, that some classes of facts, without any special effort, remained permanently fixed in their recollection, while others were as readily forgotten by them as by other men. A highly esteemed clergyman of Massachusetts, lately deceased, who could tell the year of the graduation of every alumnus of his university, and the minutest incidents relating to every ordination in his vicinity for the last half century, assured me that it cost him no labor, but that it was, so far as he knew, a mental peculiarity.

"The large development of any particular form of memory is not, of necessity, accompanied by any other remarkable intellectual endowments. Instances have frequently been noticed of men with prodigious powers of recollection, whose abilities in other respects were even below mediocrity. Very remarkable memory has even been observed in persons of so infirm an understanding, that they did not even comprehend what they accurately repeated. In this case, probably, the power was mere susceptibility of memory; that is, the power of acquiring on the instant, without the ability of permanent recollection. A very remarkable case of this one-sided power is mentioned in the life of the late Mr. Roscoe, of Liverpool. A young Welsh fisherman, of about the age of eighteen, was found to have made most remarkable progress in the study of languages. He was not only familiar with Latin and Greek, but also with Hebrew, Arabic, and other Oriental dialects. Some benevolent gentlemen in that city provided means for giving him every literary advantage, in the hope that his vast acquisitions might be made useful to society, and also that he might unfold the processes by which his singular attainments had been made. The attempt was, however, unsuccessful. He seemed not to be peculiarly capable of education, but, with the exception of this peculiar gift, his mind partook entirely of the character of the class with which he had been associated."

On the other hand, it is rare that high intellectual powers are found in connection with a defective memory. "For intellectual power of the highest order," says Hamilton, "none were distinguished above Grotius and Pascal; and Grotius and Pascal forgot nothing they had ever read or thought. Leibnitz and Euler were not less celebrated for their intelligence than for their memory, and both could repeat the whole of the *Æneid*. Donellus knew the *Corpus Juris* by neart, and yet he was one of the profoundest and most original speculators in jurisprudence. Muratori, though not a genius of the very highest order, was still a man of great ability and judgment; and so powerful was his retention, that in making quotations he had only to read his passages, put the books in their place, and then to write out from memory the words. Ben Jonson tells us that he could repeat all he had ever written, and whole books that he had read. Themistocles could call by their names the twenty thousand citizens of Athens; Cyrus is reported to have known the names of every soldier in his army. Hortensius, after Cicero the greatest orator of Rome, after sitting a whole day at a public sale, correctly enunciated from memory all the things sold, their prices, and the names of the purchasers. Niebuhr, the historian of Rome, was not less distinguished for his memory than for his acuteness. In his youth he was employed in one of the public offices of Denmark; part of a book of accounts having been destroyed, he restored it from his recollection. Sir James Mackintosh was, likewise, remarkable for his power of memory. An instance I can give you which I witnessed myself. In a conversation I had with him, we happened to touch upon an author whom I mentioned in my last lecture—Muretus; and Sir James recited from his oration in praise of the massacre of St. Bartholomew some considerable passages. Mr. Dugald Stewart, and the late Dr. Gregory, are likewise examples of great talent united with great memory."

As there has been thought to be an incompatibility between great powers of memory and a sound judgment, it may be well to consider the relation of memory to judgment; that is, what relation those mental acts which we call acts of memory sustain to those mental acts which we call conclusions or judgments.

A man of good judgment draws accurate inferences from complex premises. From simple premises, men of slender capacity can draw accurate inferences. If one sees footprints on the sand, he infers that some person has been walking there. When the premises are complex—when the inference is to be drawn from a variety of facts, some of them obscure, perhaps, and some of them apparently in conflict, there is difficulty and liability to error. A man who cognizes the truth —draws accurate conclusions—under such circumstances, is called a man of good judgment.

The various facts from which he draws his inferences must be viewed, not separately, but in their relations to each other. This comprehensive view requires the exercise of memory. The facts must be clearly before the mind, either by direct seeing or distinct remembrance. Besides, the final conclusion must be the result of many subordinate conclusions. Hence they must all be distinctly remembered. Unless a man, therefore, have a good memory, he cannot be a man of good judgment. He may not have a good memory for dates and casual occurrences; but he must have a good memory in relation to the materials of his reasonings. He must have a good memory in relation to trains of thought.

The power of memory is early developed, and, in comparison with the other powers, early decays. The first indications of mental decline have respect to the memory. The aged man forgets recent events. He forgets the events of yesterday, while he remembers the events of childhood. Why is this?

It is said that events in early life make a deeper impression upon the memory than events in later life, and are therefore remembered. Is this apparent reason for the fact any more than a re-affirmance of the fact in other words? The careful observer will meet with many examples of this method of procedure, when attempts are made to give a reason for that for which no reason can be given. Does the mind ever forget any of its experiences? Are any mental operations so entirely forgotten that they cannot be recalled?

"From remarkable and well authenticated facts," says Dr. Wayland, "it appears that, probably from some unexplained condition of the material organs, the recollection of knowledge long since obliterated may be suddenly revived. These cases have been observed to occur most frequently in extreme sickness, and on the near approach of death. May it not be that, in our present state, the material and immaterial part of man being intimately united, our failure of recollection is caused by some condition of the material organism; and that, as this union approaches dissolution, the power of the material over the immaterial is weakened, and the knowledge which we have once acquired is more fully revealed to our consciousness, indicating that when the separation is complete it will remain with us forever?

"A variety of cases are mentioned by writers on this subject, a few of which are here inserted.

"An instance is mentioned by Coleridge of a servant-girl in Germany, who, in extreme sickness, was observed to repeat passages of Greek, Latin, and Hebrew, though she was known to have no acquaintance with those languages. Upon inquiry into her history, it was found that many years before, she had been a domestic in the family of a learned professor, who was in the habit of repeating aloud passages from his favorite authors while walking in his study, which adjoined the apartment in which she was accustomed to labor. This case is the more remarkable, inasmuch as the person had never been conscious herself of having acquired the knowledge which she, under these circumstances, exhibited.

"The Rev. Mr. Flint, a very intelligent gentleman, who, in a series of interesting letters, has related his experiences in the valley of the Mississippi, informs us that, under a desperate attack of typhus fever, as his attendants afterwards told him, he repeated whole pages from Virgil and Homer, which he had never committed to memory, and of which, after his recovery, he could not recollect a line.

"Dr. Abercrombie, in his work on intellectual philosophy, mentions a variety of cases in which persons in extreme sickness, and under operations for injuries of the head, conversed in languages which they had known in youth, but had for many years entirely forgotten.

"Dr. Rush mentions the case of an Italian gentleman who died of yellow fever in New York, who, in the beginning of his sickness, spoke English; in the middle of it, French; but on the day of his death, nothing but Italian. A Lutheran clergyman informed Dr. Rush that the Germans and Swedes of his congregation in Philadelphia, when near death, always prayed in their native languages, though some of them, he was confident, had not spoken them for fifty or sixty years.

"Dr. Abercrombie mentions another case, of a boy, who, at the age of four, received a fracture of the skull, for which he underwent the operation of the trepan. He was at the time in a state of perfect stupor; and, after his recovery, retained no recollection either of the accident or of the operation. At the age of fifteen, during the delirium of a fever, he gave his mother a correct description of the operation, and the persons who were present at it, with their dress and other minute particulars. He had never been observed to allude to it before, and no means were known by which he could have acquired a knowledge of the circumstances which he related.

"What conclusion we are authorized to draw from these facts, it is difficult to determine. They, however, indicate that what we seem to forget can never be irretrievably lost to the percipient soul. The means for recalling it in some inexplicable manner appears to exist; and when, under some unknown conditions, they are called into action, all or any part of our knowledge may on the instant be brought to our recollection.

"The moral lesson which these facts inculcate is obvious. If every impression made upon the mind is to remain upon it forever; if the soul be a tablet from which nothing that is written is ever erased, how great is the importance of imbuing it with that knowledge which shall be a source of joy to us as long as we exist. And, again, since knowledge which lies so long dormant may be revived unexpectedly, under conditions which we cannot foresee, and at times when it may have the most important bearings upon our decisions and our destiny, it is of the greatest consequence to us to store the mind with such knowledge as shall invigorate our principles and confirm our virtue. He who reads a corrupting book for pastime may thoughtlessly lay it down, and suppose that in a few days all the images which it has created will have passed from his remembrance forever. But these latent ideas may be recalled by some casual association, or some physical condition of the brain, and give that bias to his mind in the hour of temptation, which will determine him to a course that shall tend to his final undoing."

The power of memory is susceptible of rapid and great improvement; and as many of the most important of the operations of the mind are conditioned upon its proper exercise, it is worthy of cultivation. The law of its growth is exercise, and the only difficulty lying in the way is indolence. Every fact, every thought perfectly mastered, increases the power of the memory. The memory is not like a storehouse, which may be filled to repletion. It is a power that grows strong in proportion to the amount of work it does. The more one remembers accurately and perfectly, the more he can remember. Few, if any, acquire the power of memory which they might acquire.

There is in the minds of some a prejudice against committing to memory *verbatim;* but the power of so doing is very desirable, and almost indispensable. No power of retaining what is called the substance of a discourse or chapter will supply its place. What is wanted is power to remember thoughts in their connection, and words also. In early life, the mind should be exercised much in committing to memory. The habit thus formed will be of great importance in subsequent life. It is not, of course, to be a substitute for the exercise of other powers, but a condition for the exercise of those powers. If those teachers who rigidly exact the accurate exercise of the memory, would in like manner exact a rigid exercise of the reasoning power, there would be no prejudices against their pupils in consequence of their power of memory. They would not be termed men of mere memory.

As Dr. Wayland remarks, "The importance of this faculty is frequently underrated, especially by young men. If a man succeed in almost any department of intellectual labor, it is often said, by way of disparagement, that his effort is nothing but the result of unusual memory. Were this the fact, it would still be true that the cultivation of memory to high perfection, so that our past knowledge is always available in every emergency, is neither an ordinary nor a contemptible attainment. But the assertion is commonly unfounded. While distinguished success in any department can rarely be attained by the exercise of memory alone, it is equally true that the noblest powers would be continually liable to mortifying failure without it. Let us, then, labor to cultivate this faculty by every means in our power, always remembering that we shall derive from it the greatest advantage, not by allowing it to supersede the use of the other faculties, but by training it to act in subordination to them. He who reasons without facts must always proceed in the dark; while he who relies on isolated facts, neither using his powers of generalization nor reasoning, must be willing to remain always a child."

Is memory to be trusted? Can we rely upon our recollections? It is said that memory sometimes deceives us: how, then, can we be sure that in any given instance it does not deceive us? If a witness is known to testify falsely sometimes, how can we be sure that he testifies truly at any given time, unless there is other evidence to the truth of what he affirms?

The attentive reader will readily see that there is no analogy between mistakes in regard to remembering and false testimony on the part of a witness.

What is meant by the expression, Our memory sometimes deceives us? Simply that we sometimes think we remember a thing when we do not remember it; just as we sometimes think we see a thing when we do not see it. The fact that sometimes, in a mist, we mistake a shrub for a man, does not cause us to doubt whether we see the man that stands before us in the clear sunlight. There are some things which we are absolutely certain we see; so there are some things which we are absolutely certain we remember. Trusting our memories is trusting our minds. We can trust our minds in regard to our recollections as well as in regard to our perceptions.

CHAPTER XXIV.

ASSOCIATION.

IN all our waking hours we are conscious of a constant succession of thoughts and feelings. We can influence the train of thought by turning our attention to certain objects, and withdrawing it from other objects; but when we make no such effort, the train proceeds spontaneously. The thoughts do not, however, succeed each other at random, but according to certain laws, or certain relations existing between them. The relations most influential are those of resemblance, contrast, contiguity in time or place, and cause and effect. These are commonly called laws of association. They are facts derived from experience.

Thoughts have a tendency to introduce resembling thoughts, or are naturally followed by resembling thoughts. You see a building: you remember one similar to it. You read a beautiful passage: you remember a similar one. The suggesting similarity between two things may relate to the things themselves, or to their causes, or to their consequences.

The resemblance may be striking, or it may be slight. Dr. Thomas Brown affirms that genius consists in the capacity of associating ideas by remote analogies.

Thoughts have a tendency to introduce their opposites. The palace suggests the hovel, the desert the luxuriant field. The rhetorical figure of antithesis is founded on the principle of contrast. Fewer thoughts are introduced by this relation than by the relation of resemblance.

When we visit the scenes of our childhood, the incidents of that period are brought to mind. We never think of Thermopylæ without thinking of Leonidas. We never think of Calvary without thinking of the stupendous event of which it was the scene. Places owe their chief interest to the events associated with them. Contiguity in time and place is a principle of association in all minds, and a leading one in uneducated minds.

When we see an event, we think of its cause and of its consequences. This principle of association is prominent in philosophical minds.

The above-mentioned relations have a great influence in determining our trains of thought; yet other relations have an influence. The relations between our thoughts are numberless, and any one of them may introduce a thought. Some have attempted to enumerate all the laws of association, and have enumerated primary and secondary laws—objective and subjective laws. To enumerate all the facts that may cause one thought to introduce another, would be to enumerate all the relations existing between our thoughts; and that is impossible.

Our spontaneous trains of thought are modified by the peculiar emotive condition of the mind. Different laws of association operate in different moods of mind. When the mind is in a gloomy state, a joyous assembly may suggest a funeral: when in a cheerful state, it calls to remembrance a similar assembly. In the one case the principle of contrast, and in the other that of similitude, determines the suggestion.

While our trains of thought are thus dependent upon relations which we do not create, yet they are not beyond our control. We can cause our thoughts to succeed each other in accordance with certain relations rather than others. We can put our minds in an attitude favorable to the operation of a particular law. The more our thoughts succeed each other according to that law, the greater will be their tendency to do so. In this way, in the case of the poet, the law of resemblance and of contrast becomes prominent, and in the case of the philosopher, the law of cause and effect.

"The will," says Dr. Hickok, "may have much to do in regulating and controlling the association of thought, and an earnest and protracted effort may cultivate and discipline this faculty in various directions. A man may make himself a rhymer, a punster, a dealer in charades and anagrams, by certain habits of associating thoughts with words; or observing, inventive, practically effective, by certain associations of thoughts with things. An orderly and methodical train of thought may be cultivated by keeping the operation of this faculty under the regulations of time, place, and circumstance, so that the thought may be appropriate to the occasion."

Some writers have treated this subject in a manner that has led to erroneous conclusions. They have regarded the mind as wholly passive in respect to its trains of thought—as helplessly subject to the laws of association. Our trains of thought, it is said, do not depend upon our wills, but upon laws ordained by a higher power. We are therefore not responsible for them, nor for the conclusions to which they lead us. Thus man is not responsible for his belief. He may be an infidel and not be to blame for it. Dr. Thomas Brown and Lord Brougham teach that men are not responsible for their opinions. And there is a popular prejudice which regards freedom of opinion as inconsistent with responsibility for belief.

It is true that belief is not under the direct control of the will. We cannot believe a proposition by willing to believe it. Belief depends upon evidence. We can attend to the evidence of a proposition; we can guard against the influence of prejudice. If the evidence is adequate, belief follows. Our belief is thus indirectly under our control. A direct control over all our states of mind is not a necessary condition of responsibility for our belief.

We are responsible for the right exercise of our minds; and the right exercise of our minds will result in the formation of correct opinions.

We are responsible for our actions, and we are under obligation to act rationally. If we act rationally, we shall act in accordance with our views of truth—that is, with our opinions; hence the responsibility reaches back to our opinions.

God holds us responsible for our opinions. He requires us to believe the truth, to form correct opinions. This is taught throughout the Bible.

The law of resemblance suggests an important mode of procedure in respect to self-culture. When we store the mind with choice thoughts, they will, by the law of resemblance, introduce similar ones. Hence we should become familiar with the best thoughts of the best authors. This explains, in part at least, the fact of mental assimilation. We become like those with whose works we are familiar.

The laws of association are sometimes considered under the head of memory, as though they operated only in reviving thoughts that have been experienced. This is not the case. If we may be said to remember by association, we may be said to reason by association. The laws of association often bring to our minds thoughts that were never there before.

Suppose one is engaged in the work of original composition. He designs to prove a particular proposition. The thoughts which constitute that proof are not present to his mind. He cannot directly will their presence—that would be to have them already. He fixes his attention on the proposition. He watches for thoughts which tend to his purpose. From the ceaseless flow of thoughts, he selects such as seem suited to his purpose. These introduce others of like tendency. By degrees the materials for his proof are selected. The train from which they were selected was in accordance with the laws of association modified by his will—just as is the case in voluntary recollection.

In this case, thoughts which were never in the mind before, are introduced by the same laws or relations which call up thoughts that had formerly been in the mind.

Association is therefore not properly termed a faculty. It denotes a mode of the mind's operation with respect to several of its faculties. It is true, we define a faculty to be a mode of the mind's operation: association is a mode of the mind's operation, but not in the sense in which we use that phrase when we would designate a faculty. Associated thoughts form a portion of the operations classed under the head of memory, of reasoning, of imagination, of the æsthetic and moral faculties. Association is a term expressive of our thoughts as successive and related.

A knowledge of the principles of association is specially important to the dramatist, the writer of fiction, and the critic. The dramatist and novelist form ideal characters which are represented as speaking and acting. Their language and actions must be in keeping with their characters. The characters must be natural, and their language and action in accordance with the natural laws of thought and feeling. The facts connected with association must therefore be known to the author. The same is true of the critic, whose office is to sit in judgment on the productions of the author. One important question he is to decide is, Are the characters and incidents of the work natural—that is, in accordance with the laws of thought and feeling? A knowledge of those laws is a necessary condition of an intelligent decision.

The principle of habit is usually referred to association. The law or fact which underlies habit is not strictly a law of association, yet it is one of great importance.

The repetition of an act increases the tendency to the performance of that act, and increased facility in performing it. Repetition continued at stated intervals forms a habit, which is a condition of mind disposing to perform certain acts, and giving facility in the performance of said acts. A habit may be grafted on an original disposition, or it may be wholly factitious. The chief object of education is the formation of right mental habits.

Habits are active or passive. One may form a habit of industry or a habit of indolence. The one is formed by action, the other by inaction.

A course of action which is unpleasant at first, becomes pleasant when habitual. Labor is not in itself pleasant to many, if indeed it be to any; but habit makes it agreeable, nay, a source of high enjoyment. We have, therefore, to fix upon that course of exertion which duty requires, and habit will soon render it agreeable.

When a habit is founded on the love of some particular indulgence, the pleasure decays as the habit is formed, and the pain of want is the stimulus instead of expected pleasure.

Right habits increase our power to do right, and lessen the difficulties in our way. The constitution of our minds whereby we are rendered capable of forming habits, is thus a cause for gratitude to our Maker.

Our great business here is the formation of right habits. Right habits, so far as they are perfectly formed, render the soul perfect, and confirm it in that condition. If one were suddenly made perfectly virtuous, he would need to form habits of virtue to preserve him in that condition.

CHAPTER XXV.

IMAGINATION.

You have seen an edifice: when absent from it, you can form a mental image of it—can see it with the mind's eye. The capacity of the mind for performing this act, is termed imagination. The act is a simple one, and is thus incapable of definition. We use figurative language when we call it an image. There can be no literal resemblance between an edifice,—material object, and an act of the immaterial mind.

It may be said the image of the edifice is a remembrance, more or less perfect, of its appearance. This is true; but the image-making power is clearly distinguishable from the remembering power. This appears from the fact that we can form images of things which we have not seen. A skilful description of the edifice will enable us to form an image of it, almost as complete as if we had seen it. To remember is to recall past mental states, recognizing them as past. The process of image-making will take place in remembering according to the nature of the mental acts recalled, and the habits of the individual's mind.

We can also form images of things which never have existed. An architect forms a mental image of the edifice he is about to erect.

This image-making power has been called by some writers conception. Conception is by them defined to be the power to form an image of an object previously perceived. It is comparatively of little consequence what name is given to a mental act, so that the act be clearly stated.

Those who would designate the image-making power by the term conception, apply the term imagination to the process by which conceptions are combined into new wholes. For example, one may take conceptions of different features, and selecting one from one man and another from another, may form a new combination of features differing from any that has existed. He must select his features, which said writers call an exercise of abstraction, and combine them, and the result is a product of imagination. Imagination, they tell us, is thus a complex operation, to which abstraction, conception, and taste render their aid. The objection to this statement is, that the calling in the aid of several faculties tends to produce obscurity, if not confusion, in the reader's mind.

The operation of forming new wholes, whatever we may call those wholes, is a complex operation.

11*

Let the object be to form an image, conception, or product of imagination, different from any thing before known. Let the object be to form an imaginary castle differing from any castle that has existed. The mind selects from castles which it has seen, or heard, or read of, certain parts, and out of these parts, which exist as mental images, it forms a new whole. We cannot tell how it does this: we know that it does do it. Nothing is gained by saying that abstraction selects the materials, that judgment or taste approves the selection. In the complex operations referred to imagination, mental acts which we, when classifying mental acts, refer to separate faculties, find a place. The same is true of all complex or combined mental operations, whether they have reference to the formation of images, the discovery of truth, or its communication. An act of imagination is not the act of something separate from the mind; it is the mind acting in a particular way—putting forth peculiar acts, forming images.

The power of forming mental images is possessed by all men, but, like other powers, is not possessed by all in the same degree. Some can form distinct and vivid images of objects which they have seen, or which are described in language; others form dim and indistinct images.

Some readily form images of objects thus set before them, but are destitute of the power of forming new images. They can only repeat the processes of other minds. This has been termed a passive exercise of the imagination.

An active exercise is said to consist in forming new images, by means of the process of selection and combination above noticed.

An author is said to have a creative imagination who produces new scenes and new characters. Is it certain that the process of construction is that assumed above? Did Shakespeare, when he created a new character, take one quality from one real character and another from another, and thus form a new character out of old materials? To answer this question by an appeal to consciousness, it would be necessary to have the consciousness of one possessing a creative imagination. May not the mind possess a power more strictly analogous to the creative? In the origination of a new character, may not the process be that of construction from analogy—not that of selection and combination? May there not be a difference between a combination of cognized parts into a new whole, and the production of a new whole analogous to something previously known?

One man studies a picture. He makes a copy of it, or changes it by introducing some parts from another picture. Another studies the same picture. Conceptions are awakened which he throws upon the canvas. His work is not made up of parts of the pictures studied, and yet it was occasioned by the study of them. May we not safely affirm that the original productions of the mind referred to imagination are more nearly allied to the creative than to the formative? I am aware that this is not pointing out in what the distinction consists.

The power of imagination is not to be confounded with the power to cognize beauty. In order to form beautiful imaginative creations, there must be the power of cognizing beauty; but the power to cognize beauty may be possessed by one who has little or no power of imagination, formative or creative.

One who abounds in the use of figures is said to have a fine imagination, whereas his characteristic power is that of cognizing analogies. With it is probably always connected the power of forming mental images, but not of necessity the power of producing new combinations. When Burke's gorgeous imagination is spoken of, reference is had to his power of cognizing analogies. Analogies are cognized, not created. A man looks upon the fading leaf, and exclaims, "We all do fade as a leaf." He sees an analogy. He creates nothing. The act is cognitive, not imaginative.

The forming a mental image of a visible object is the act which gives designation to the power under consideration. There are other acts, by no means identical with it, referred to the same power. We form an imaginary character. Grant that it is made up of traits selected from characters known to us, yet the conceptions of those traits are not images in the sense in which our conception of St. Peter's is an image. A conception of a character differs from a conception of a landscape. The idea of the picturable enters into the one, and not into the other.

An imaginary conversation is held. There may be images of persons supposed to be conversing, but there are no images of the sentences supposed to be uttered.

We thus apply the term imaginary to things unreal as distinguishable from real: we do not confine the term to the picturable.

Poetry and fiction are said to be the products of imagination. By this is meant, that acts which we term acts of imagination have a prominent place in said works. The plan of a work of fiction, its characters and incidents, may be imaginary—that is, the mental acts expressed in language are those that we refer to the head of imagination; but much of the filling up of the plot may consist of acts that we refer to other heads. Sound reasoning, admirable illustrations of important principles, are found in works termed works of imagination. Poetry is not necessarily the product of imagination. There are scenes in nature, an accurate description of which—an accurate statement of the truth in relation to which—constitutes poetry. The poetry of a stanza or stanzas may consist of the expression of a fine analogy. There are human actions, the simple record of which constitutes poetry.

There are operations far removed from poetry and

fiction, in which acts of imagination have a prominent place. A military commander forms his plan of a campaign. He has a mental image of the country which is the theatre of war, of his own army and that of the enemy, and of the movements which will probably be made. He fights imaginary battles, and conducts an imaginary campaign. Here is a series of mental operations of great importance, tending to great practical results. Of this series, processes that are legitimately referable to imagination form an essential part. The series abounds with sound reasonings, but they are founded on supposititious or imaginary events. A good imagination may be said to be essential to a great military commander.

The same is true of all men of enterprise and forecast. Plans having reference to the future call into exercise the constructive power of the mind as truly as did the composition of "Paradise Lost." In such cases there is no call for the æsthetic element. A man may be a great general and a great man of business without having the power of perceiving beauty.

Hypotheses are imaginary solutions of scientific questions, and have often been formed as the guides of experiment. If experiment proves the hypothesis to be true, the hypothesis becomes a theory. Imagination has, therefore, much to do with scientific progress.

Imagination is most important with respect to models; that is, the mental operation of forming models is most important. No one in any department of effort attains an excellence transcending his conception of excellence. He always comes short of it. In the fine arts, the artist never realizes the full beauty of his ideal. The artist has his model— his conception of excellence. To realize it on the canvas, or in marble, or in the anthem, is the object of his effort. He who cannot form a conception of high excellence can never become an original artist. He can be only a copyist, an imitator.

The painter or sculptor repairs to those portions of the world where the most perfect specimens of art are to be found. These specimens he studies, not that he may imitate them, but that he may be aided in forming conceptions, models, to which he may give a local habitation and a name.

The importance of models is not confined to the fine arts. They have their place in every department of human effort where excellence is sought. Especially are they important in the most important of all arts, the art of forming a strong, beautiful, and holy mind.

Every student should form a true conception of excellence in regard to character and attainment. One of the great advantages of biography is to enable us to form models of excellence, to the realization of which our efforts should be directed.

The importance of models in relation to the formation of character appears from the fact, that one object of Christ's mission was to furnish a perfect model of human excellence—a conception that no man before His time ever attained. There is no proof that the idea of a perfect manhood was ever possessed by any one who did not derive it from a knowledge of the character of Christ. In all our efforts at self-improvement, regard should be had to the perfect model set before us in the character of Christ. To neglect this model when aiming at excellence of character, were more unwise than to close our eyes on the beauty of nature when attempting to improve our power of cognizing beauty.

The legitimate operations of imagination are attended with enjoyment and profit. Even the perversion of this power is attended with enjoyment. The day-dreamer is happy for the time being.

Hence, imagination should receive proper culture in the work of self-improvement. The imagination is cultivated, as memory and the reasoning faculties are cultivated, by exercise. The mind performs the process of reasoning more readily in proportion as it is exercised in reasoning. The mind performs the process of imagining the more readily in proportion as it is exercised in imagining.

How shall it be exercised? By reading works of imagination, by forming wise plans and scientific hypotheses.

It is supposed by some that the chief exercise of the imagination consists in reading works of fiction,

In regard to a vast number of such works, they contain very little that can be legitimately said to be the product of imagination. There are few writers of creative power. The works of such writers only are worthy of being read. The works of such writers, unless they contain moral poison, will always be read with profit.

The mind grows by intimate communion with superior minds. Intimacy with a man of genius, personally or by his works, will promote mental improvement. Who ever read and understood Shakespeare, Milton, Bunyan, Dickens, and Thackeray, without receiving not merely amusement, but mental profit?

We cannot associate habitually with feeble minds without injury to ourselves. We cannot become familiar with the works of feeble minds without injury. The mass of fiction with which the press groans is for the most part the product of feeble minds, and hence should be avoided altogether.

"We may cultivate the imagination," says Dr. Wayland, "by studying attentively works most distinguished for poetical combination. I say study attentively, in distinction from the mere cursory perusal of classical authors. We must not only read, but meditate on the sublime and beautiful in thought, until we feel the full force of every analogy, entering into the spirit of the writer himself, if we would avail ourselves of the most successful efforts of human genius. We thus acquire the intellectual habits of the masters of human thought. In the language of poetry we catch a portion of their inspiration, instead of servilely rendering their thoughts in our own language. It is by a diligent study of a few of the best writers, and not the hasty reading of many, that we derive the greatest benefit from the study of the classics of our own or any other country." These remarks have reference to mental culture in general, as well as to imagination.

The propriety of using fiction as the vehicle of truth, is settled by the example of Christ. The parables of the New Testament furnish the requisite authority for those who, like Bunyan, would use the gifts of imagination bestowed upon them in teaching and enforcing truth.

Some seem to suppose that high powers of imagination and of reasoning are incompatible. We have thus far seen nothing in the character of the operations classed under the heads of imagination and reasoning which would show any incompatibility. So far is this prejudice from being true, it may safely be affirmed that the right cultivation of one faculty has a tendency to strengthen all the faculties. This is only saying that the legitimate action of the mind in one class of operations, quickens its power to perform other operations. The legitimate use of the axe strengthens the arm to use the plane.

The term fancy has been employed in several

meanings. With Stewart it is the power of cognizing analogies. "It is," says he, "the power of fancy which supplies the poet with metaphorical language, and with all the analogies which are the foundation of his allusions. But it is the power of imagination which creates the complex scenes he describes, and the fictitious characters which he delineates."

Some of the German writers give the name fancy to the spontaneous exercise of imagination—spontaneous as distinguished from voluntary.

I think the prevailing usage of the term fancy is to express the lighter forms of imagination. A scheme or plan which is but remotely analogous to truth, which pays but little regard to the natural, is said to be a fanciful scheme. The productions of an ill-regulated imagination would often be termed fanciful.

Some operations are improperly ascribed to the imagination. It is said that a man passing through a graveyard at night imagined that he saw a ghost. What were the facts of the case? He saw a white rose in bloom, and under the influence of fear inferred that it was a ghost. His error was a false conclusion from a sense-perception.

A man imagines that he has been slighted, when he has not. He has drawn a conclusion that the facts in regard to his treatment did not warrant.

A well-developed imagination is a source of enjoyment and of power. We cognize truth in the concrete, not in the abstract. We arrive at general truths by means of individual truths. The dramatist, the writer of imaginary histories, has it in his power to communicate truth more effectively than the philosopher.

CHAPTER XXVI.

THE WILL.

The will is the mind willing—not a separate agent, as the language often used respecting it would imply. It has been called the executive faculty, and the attributes of personality have been assigned to it. To such an extent has this been the case, that it is difficult to think on this subject without regarding the will as an entity controlling the mind. Let it be remembered that by the voluntary faculty, or the will, we mean simply the capacity of the mind to perform acts of volition; just as by memory we mean the capacity of the mind to recall past thoughts and feelings. An act of the will is an act of the mind—the mind willing or performing an act of volition. We must guard against the impression that the will is an agent separate from the mind, and controlling its acts.

The mind, then, has the power of performing acts of volition. A volition cannot be defined. It is a simple act, and is known only in consciousness. You will to move your arm; the motion takes place. The volition causing the motion is clearly defined in consciousness, though it cannot be in language.

Volitions sustain important relations to other mental acts. They are conditioned on other acts or states of mind, and influence succeeding acts or states.

Volition is always preceded by desire. Desire is a simple feeling known in consciousness, but incapable of analysis or definition. Consciousness testifies that every volition is preceded by some desire. Contemplate any volition of which you have been conscious. Why did you put forth that volition? You will find that some desire occasioned it.

If you doubt the truth of the affirmation, if you think the mind can will without having any desire whatever to do so, make the experiment; perform an act of will without any antecedent desire: you will probably find yourself in the condition of a pupil who stoutly contended that he could put forth a volition without any antecedent desire if *he had a mind to.*

There is in consciousness a plain distinction between the state of mind termed desire and the state of mind termed volition, though some writers regard them as identical. It is thought that some difficulties are avoided by regarding them as identical. But we should consult consciousness, and abide by its decisions—not departing from them in the vain hope of avoiding difficulties.

A man desires to take a journey. The desire may be felt for years before the will to take the journey is put forth. Those who regard desire and volition as identical, say that what we call volition is simply an intense form of the desire. It is true that the desire may become gradually or suddenly more intense, and the consequence may be a volition; but the volition is clearly distinguishable in consciousness from the desire. No man ever mistook a desire for his dinner, however great that desire, for the act of willing to eat.

Will it be said that we sometimes will in opposition to desire? The error implied in this assertion arises from failing to distinguish between two desires that may be felt at the same time. Let us consider an example of willing in opposition to desire. A child has no desire to go to school, and yet he goes: of course he wills to go. Does he will to go in opposition to his desire? He wills in opposition to his desire to stay at home or go to the play-ground, but not in opposition to his desire to avoid punishment which might follow truancy. Let the question, "Why did he go?" be answered. It will be found that he was influenced by some motive—a desire to please his parents, or to avoid punishment, or a sense of duty.

The mind is free in willing. No material restraint is laid upon it. No mental restraint is laid upon it. The mind is conscious when it wills that it exercises freedom.

What is meant by freedom of will—the theme

of so much discussion? It may be replied, The freedom of the mind in willing. If it be asked, In what does the freedom of the mind in willing consist? I do not know that any better answer can be given than that it consists in being free. To speak of the freedom of voluntariness is to speak of the freedom of freedom. Freedom with respect to mental operations, if not identical with voluntariness, is inseparable from it.

A man acts freely when he acts without constraint —when he does as he pleases. It would be a singular definition of free acting, to say that he acts freely when he does not do as he pleases. By action is meant voluntary action. In all such action, volition is the essential element. What can be affirmed of the action can be affirmed of the volition.

To act as one pleases, is to act in accordance with one's desires. The mind is free as respects volition when it can will as it desires to. That it can and does thus will, is attested by every one's consciousness.

The freedom of the mind in willing is an intuitive truth. It is seen by all who are capable of accountable action. When one says, "I feel that I am a free moral agent," he gives expression to an intuitive cognition.

Hence, that man is a free moral agent does not require proof. All arguments against it must be fallacious—as are all arguments brought against intuitive truths. Whether we can detect the fallacy or not, makes no difference as to our convictions in regard to human freedom.

It may be said, There are some who deny that the will is free—who hold to the doctrine of fatalism. Now, as it is characteristic of self-evident truths that they are admitted by all, it follows that the freedom of the will, or rather of man in willing, is not a self-evident truth.

It is true that the mark of an intuitive or self-evident fact is, that it is admitted by all either in words or by action. That the things around us are real, not mere subjective illusions, is a self-evident truth; but there are philosophers who profess to believe that they are merely subjective—there are idealists. Still, in their practical conduct, they regard a wall as a wall, and an enraged animal as a reality, and not a subjective idea. By their action they recognize the truth that the objects around us are real.

There are men who profess to disbelieve in human freedom and human accountability; but let any one appropriate the property of such men, and they will complain of the injustice done them, and demand the punishment of the offender. They thus recognize the doctrine of human freedom and human accountability.

We have seen that some desire always precedes a volition; we have seen that man wills as he pleases—that is, as he desires: does he always will in accordance with the strongest desire? Suppose there are two desires in his mind at the same time, or that they succeed each other in alternation so rapidly that, for all practical purposes, it is the same as if they were co-existent. Suppose one desire is stronger than the other: in accordance with which will the man will? Which will lead him to determine to do or not to do a certain thing, the stronger or the weaker desire? It may be said, he may follow which one he pleases. True; but which will he please to follow, the weaker or the stronger desire?

The proper method of deciding in this case, is for each one to consult his own consciousness—his own experience. Take a case in which two or more desires were felt, and a decision was to be made. Note the decision made, and which desire it was the result of. Can any one find a case in which he acted in accordance with the weaker desire—did one thing when he had a greater desire to do another practicable thing—another thing equally within his capacity for action?

It is said that we ground our assertion, that the mind wills in accordance with the strongest desire, on the fact that the act of will was performed. We are charged with saying that the desire was the strongest because volition resulted from it. Instead of this, we affirm that the mind is capable of comparing two desires, and of cognizing their relative strength. The question whether the mind is influenced to will by the stronger or feebler desire, can thus be referred to consciousness, and a definite decision can be reached.

Cannot a man act in accordance with the weaker desire, if he chooses to? Is not this choosing another form of expressing the fact that, on the whole, the so-called weaker desire is the stronger; or that the object of the supposed weaker desire is desired more than the object of the supposed stronger desire? Suppose the two objects of desire be a suit of clothes and a horse. It is readily supposable that the desire for the horse is stronger than the desire for the suit of clothes. If it be—if we know it to be so—then could we not confidently predict that he would purchase the horse? What would be the ground of our prediction? Would it not be the uniform experience that we have had, that men act according to the strongest desire?

Suppose our predictions fail to be realized: the clothes are purchased. We inquire how this came to pass, when the desire for the horse was the strongest. We learn that certain other conditions were presented to his mind: his parents expressed their disapprobation of his purpose to purchase the horse; the clothes were highly commended by one in whose taste he had confidence; these and other considerations influenced him. The combined desire to please his parents and to possess the clothes became stronger than the desire which we supposed would occasion a decision.

Observe, we do not affirm that the strongest desire governs the mind just as the heaviest weight brings down the balance. The presence of this and kindred false analogies has vitiated a great deal of the thinking that has been exercised on this subject. The mind is not a passive subject, in which desires spontaneously spring up and irresistibly control it : it is an active free agent, that can do what it has a mind to, and does do what it has a mind to.

Desires, it is true, are in their origin spontaneous; but the mind has an indirect control over them —can repress or indulge them, and can thus, in view of them, determine its own volitions.

Man' has thus a self-determining power. No being wills for him. He wills himself as he pleases. To say that the will has a self-determining power, is to say that the mind has a self-determining power. The will is nothing apart from the mind willing. The question is whether the mind determines its volitions in view of motives or without motives, or in opposition to all motives ?

What are motives ? Are they external to the mind, or internal ? A man's motives are the reasons of his conduct. Man is a reasonable being, and should have a reason for all that he does—that is, for all his voluntary actions. To act from good motives, is to be a good man ; to act from bad motives, is to be a bad man.

A man's motives, it was said, are the reasons of his conduct ; they are internal—being conscious states of mind for which he is responsible. External objects may be the occasion of producing states of mind which constitute motives. An apple may attract one's attention and awaken a desire to possess it, and that may lead to effort—acts of will. The desire to possess it was a motive. The apple itself, irrespective of the desire, cannot be a motive. What is true of the apple, is true of all objects external to the mind. They are not motives, but may be the occasion of motives. Every motive, before it causes action, takes the form of a desire. The word motive is more comprehensive than desire, and includes the states of mind which give rise and modification to desire.

Consciousness affirms that man acts from motives. We can recall no act of our own that had not some motive—was not incited by some desire. The motive may have been a very foolish one—a very frivolous desire; but some motive there was. To the question, Why did you do so? some answer can be given. Insolence may say, Because I chose to do so, or had a mind to; but something was antecedent to the deed, and connected with it.

To say that men determine their acts in view of the strongest motive, is to say that they act in accordance with the strongest desire. No state of mind influences the decision of the mind, except as it awakens a desire or desires. To say that men determine their actions in view of motives, and that they always act in accordance with the strongest motive, is simply to say that men act in accordance with their strongest desires.

There is a caricature of this doctrine which represents motives as external, and the strongest as governing the mind. Man is thus under the control of objects without him, and is as destitute of freedom as the vessel without a rudder which must go before the wind.

To avoid this conclusion, they claim for the will a self-determining power; they claim for man a power to will without motives, and in opposition to all motives. This they think essential to freedom. They admit that man usually, if not uniformly, acts from motives; but he must, they think, have power to rise above them, and act independently of them, or he cannot be free.

To this view there is the objection, that we are always conscious of acting from some motive, and always take it for granted that all other men act from motives. The moral character of acts is judged of by the motives. We proceed upon the conviction that human actions have motives, just as we proceed upon the conviction that physical events have causes.

To affirm that man must have a power to will without motives and in opposition to all motives, and yet to confess that he seldom if ever exercises that power, while he is nevertheless free, seems to be somewhat inconsistent.

'Again, to act without motive is to act without a reason. To contend, therefore, that a man must be able to act without motives in order to be free, is to contend that he must be able to act irrationally in order to be free. Wherein would a mental act, prompted by no motive whatever, differ as to rationality from the movement of a limb by galvanism?

This view is a false inference from a fact of consciousness—the fact of remorse. When we are conscious that we have done wrong, we are conscious of guilt; and in the consciousness of guilt is involved the consciousness that we might have acted differently. If there were no power to act differently, there could be no sense of blame. The false inference drawn from this fact is, that we might have acted differently, *all our feelings which preceded volition and all the circumstances being the same.* The error lies in assuming that our conviction that we might have acted differently, is a conviction that we might have acted differently all motives and circumstances being the same. This assumption is unwarranted.

Suppose, in a moment of passion occasioned by a false view of the conduct of another, you strike him and inflict a serious injury. In a short time you are conscious that you have done wrong. You see that there was no cause for your anger, and that, if there had been, you had no right to yield to it. You say to yourself, "I ought not to have been so hasty.

A moment's reflection would have made it plain that I was in error. I ought to have been on my guard against the impulse of passion, and controlled myself." You would feel that you could have acted differently, by having had a different state of mind—different motives. You would not feel that, had you been just as hasty, thoughtless, and unguarded as you were, you could have acted differently. The obligation to have acted differently involves the obligation to have had different motives, and does not prove that you can act without motives.

All our control over our mental operations is indirect. We cannot, by an act of mere volition, cause any thought or feeling to be present to the mind. We may will to do things adapted to cause the presence of said thought or feeling. We control our mind as we control nature, by obeying its laws.

Motives are sometimes spoken of as existing without the mind, whereas they are states of mind. These states of mind may be occasioned by external objects. When an external object awakens a desire which leads to action, that object is loosely spoken of as the impelling motive. A thief breaks into a bank, and steals a quantity of gold. The gold is said to have influenced his action. It is true that the gold presented a temptation to him; but this was in consequence of the condition of his mind. If his mind had been in a perfectly healthy moral condition, the gold would have presented no temptation. Its power over the thief was owing wholly to the thievish condition of the mind. For that condition said thief was responsible.

What is true of the gold, is true of all external objects as to their power to produce voluntary action. So far as they influence the mind in connection with volition, it is owing wholly to the subjective condition of the mind, for which consciousness asserts that we are responsible.

We are responsible for certain states of mind irrespective of the means by which they were produced. A malignant disposition is the object of moral disapprobation, whether that disposition was caused by voluntary acts or was inherited. To say that one is to blame for having a malignant disposition, is to say that he ought to have a different disposition, and that he might have a different disposition. If the disposition was born with him, how could he be without it? Here we had better confess our ignorance than deny the facts of consciousness. Some deny that we inherit from our first parents any evil dispositions, though the fact is affirmed by the Word of God, and is in keeping with universal experience.

So in regard to our volitions. We should admit the facts attested by consciousness, whether we can explain the difficulties or not. We are conscious that our volitions are preceded by desires, and that we always will in accordance with the strongest desire. In our consciousness of blame for doing a wrong act, is involved the consciousness of avoidability; that is, that we might have acted otherwise. We are conscious of a self-determining power—that is, of free self-determination in view of motives which are states of mind for which we are accountable.

In some minds there seems to be a difficulty of reconciling free volitions with any conditions whatever. Such should remember that every thing which begins to be is conditioned. Every event is conditioned on some other event. Our control over all our mental operations is a conditioned control. Our power to cognize external objects is conditioned on putting our organs in certain relations to the object. Our power to remember is conditioned on certain laws of mind. It may be our duty to have a certain thought present to our minds at a certain hour, but we cannot place it there by simply willing it. It may be our duty to cognize a certain truth, but we cannot cognize it by simply willing to cognize it. We must turn our attention to the truths on which its cognition is conditioned. It may be our duty to put forth certain volitions at a certain time, but the power to do so may be conditioned on certain states of mind. The mind's power of willing is conditioned, and yet free. The fact that events are conditioned does not prove that they are the result of fatal necessity.

The doctrine set forth in these pages makes our volitions dependent upon our dispositions and character. Dr. Hickok remarks: "There is in all men a deep consciousness that, somehow, there is an alternative to present disposition and character, and thus an avoidability in all voluntary action."

Whether we are able to explain the "somehow" or not, let us admit the testimony of consciousness.

The impression that the doctrine of the strongest motive—that is, the doctrine that the mind determines to act or not to act in view of motives, or in accordance with the strongest desire—is inconsistent with freedom of will, is very strong on the minds of some able thinkers, and has led them to seek for means of avoiding the supposed difficulty. Very few such men have failed to see and acknowledge the absurdity of volitions without motives and in opposition to motives, and yet they have found motives in their way, and have sought, as it were, to get rid of them.

McCosh admits that volitions have causes, but would seem to deny that the causes of volitions are found in antecedent dispositions and desires. He says: "We hold—we cannot but hold—that the principle of cause and effect reigns in mind as in matter. Our intuitive belief in causation leads us to this conclusion. It is on account of the existence of such a connection that we can anticipate the future in regard to the actions of intelligent and voluntary beings, as well as in regard to changes in material substances. It is upon it that we ground our confidence in the character and word of God. But there is an important difference between the manner in which this principle operates in body and spirit. In all proper mental operations, the causes and the effects both lie within the mind. Mind is a self-acting substance, and hence its activity and independence."

He proceeds to give his idea of cause in connection with mental phenomena: "The true cause of any given mental phenomenon, its unconditional antecedent, which always will produce it, and without which it cannot recur, is composed of two things—the immediately preceding state, and a mental power or faculty."

In case of a volition, then, the cause would be the immediately preceding state of mind, and the mental power or faculty of will. He would probably admit that the immediately preceding state of mind was a desire. We have then a desire as one element of the cause, and the will as the other. The will, be it remembered, is simply the name given to the capacity of the mind for willing. The will in action is the mind willing. Why is this power exercised? Why is this element of the cause active instead of latent? Is it owing to the presence of the desire? If so, is not this admitting that the mind wills under the incentive of desire?

But he does not admit this conclusion. He says: "Now, we hold it to be an incontrovertible fact, and one of great importance, that the true determining cause in every given volition is not a mere anterior excitement, but the very soul itself by its inherent power of will."

No doubt the soul or mind wills—determines its own volitions; but why does it determine to put forth now sinful volitions, and now holy ones? What is the cause of the difference? Does it consist "in the inherent power of the will"? Does that phrase express any thing more than the fact that the mind can will? To say that the mind can will, is not to answer the question, Why does the mind will thus and so?

In the following passage he seems to admit the doctrine of a non-rational self-determining power:

"We must ever hold that a mere incitement can become a motive only so far as sanctioned by the will; so that it is not so much the incentive that determines the will, as the will that adopts the incentive."

Why does the will—or the mind willing—adopt one incentive rather than another? In so doing, does it act arbitrarily, without any reason—without any motive?

Will it be said, Because it chooses to? Why does it choose to? The expression, the mind wills in a particular way because it chooses to, must mean either that it wills because it wills, or that it wills because it desires to.

Wherein does sanctioning a motive differ from acting in view of it, or at its promptings? Is there any distinction in consciousness between sanctioning an incentive, and acting in accordance with it?

Dr. McCosh rarely mistakes words for things, as he seems to have done in endeavoring to avoid the supposed difficulty attendant upon the doctrine that the mind always puts forth volition in accordance with the strongest motive. May not his error arise from attempting to seek for profoundness where the truth is very simple? Do not all men, learned and unlearned, act on the principle that men will be governed by the strongest motive?

Let it be remembered that there is no analogy between the influence of a motive on the mind, and the influence of a weight on a balance. A motive is as different from a weight as a balance is from a mind. We are obliged to use figurative language when describing mental operations; but the borrowed terms should not be allowed to give us a distorted view of the facts they are borrowed to express. This has been the case in regard to the matter under consideration.

Nothing is gained, so far as we can see, by ascribing the will to *the spiritual* in man. All the thoughts, and feelings, and acts of which we are conscious, are the thoughts, and feelings, and acts of the human spirit. Some of its operations are conditioned upon its connection with the body, some of them have relation to material realities, and some to spiritual realities. It has not yet been shown that the mind, when acting in relation to spiritual realities, does not proceed on the same principles as when acting in relation to material realities. Motives drawn from the spiritual ought to have more weight than motives drawn from the material. When they do not, it is owing to the moral condition of the soul—" the spiritual disposition"

CHAPTER XXVII.

ATTENTION.

THE subject of attention has been frequently noticed in the foregoing pages. Every one knows what attention is, though few possess the power of attention in a high degree: few have the power of fixing the mind upon an unattractive subject, and of keeping it fixed till the end aimed at is gained.

Attention has been treated by some writers as a separate faculty: so far as we are conscious of effort in relation to attention, the effort is a voluntary one—is an act of will.

It is of little consequence whether we regard it as a separate faculty, or as a form of volition; but it is of the utmost consequence that power of attention be acquired.

No object can be seen unless the eyes are turned towards it. No spiritual truth can be seen, no proposition cognized, no complex subject understood, unless the mind be fixed steadily and continuously upon it.

It must be remembered that the thinker does not create truth; he only sees it. The original thinker simply sees truths that have not been seen before. Truths are seen by looking at them—fixing the attention exclusively upon them. Subjects are not comprehended by a single mental glance. Long-continued thoughtfulness—meditation—which consists mainly in fixing the attention upon them, is necessary.

The student's first efforts at attention are not remarkably successful. He opens an argumentative work, and resolves to master the arguments. He begins to read with a vigorous effort at attention. Before he has reached the bottom of the page, perhaps before he has reached the third sentence, he finds his attention wandering to other objects. He has read the words, perhaps pronounced them aloud, but has no idea of the thoughts they were intended to express. He begins again, but soon finds his attention turned towards objects far removed from the train of thought before him. After a score of efforts, perhaps, he is able to keep his attention fixed till he has reached the bottom of the page. If he will faithfully persevere in this course, he will ultimately be able to attend to a long argument as easily as he now attends to an attractive narrative.

In all his studies, the student should have reference to forming the habit of attention. No exercise is more conducive to this than analyzing works of thought. Various other advantages will result from that exercise.

Let the student select, say, an argumentative oration of Daniel Webster, or the work of some first-rate mind; and let him read with the purpose of seizing the outline of the plan—the frame-work of the discourse. Let him fix his attention on the successive thoughts which constitute the train, noting the relation of each one to that which follows. Let him endeavor to remember each thought by its relation to that which preceded it, and not by associating it with certain forms of expression, or the place which it occupies on the printed page. Let the successive thoughts be thus noticed and remembered at the expense of as few perusals as possible. Let the successive steps be mentally reviewed frequently, now by a condensed statement of each point in the train, and now by a statement, not of the thoughts, but of the relations they sustain to each other. This last will compel attention to the thoughts dissociated from the language in which they are expressed. Suppose, for example, the analysis be on this wise. First there is an introductory remark, then a statement of the proposition, then an argument from analogy in support of it, then an illustration drawn from history, then an inference from the proposition. Perfect thoroughness is thus secured, and the habit of seizing and retaining trains of thought formed.

The discipline thus secured will enable the student to arrange in his mind trains of his own construction, and keep them as steadily before his mind as if they were on paper. This power is indispensable to the extempore speaker. The extempore speaker who speaks with power, does not utter that which occurs to him after he has risen to speak; he utters that which he has pre-composed mentally. True, a man should acquire the power of "thinking on his legs,"— of speaking to the point on questions which it was impossible for him to premeditate.

Some of the most eminent public speakers not only arrange their trains of thought mentally, but even compose the sentences. Robert Hall's celebrated discourse on infidelity was thus pre-composed, and the orations of Daniel Webster give abundant proof that he possessed and practised this power.

The exercise of attention is the condition of clear apprehension, and is scarcely distinguishable from it. We have seen that it is the condition of accurate remembering. Clear apprehension and accurate remembrance are essential to sound reasoning.

Sir Isaac Newton ascribed his success to fixed and patient attention. Profound investigation is little more than concentrated, long-continued attention. The power of attention is therefore worthy of assiduous cultivation.

CHAPTER XXVIII.

TRUTH—UNDERSTANDING AND REASON—FAITH AND
REASON—INFINITY.

WE have seen that no definition can be given of truth. Every one whose mind is in a normal state knows what truth is, or rather knows what true propositions are. There are different kinds of truth; that is, there are true propositions relating to different classes of objects. There are truths material, spiritual, æsthetic, moral, etc. Some truths are contingent and some are necessary. It is true that there is such a place as Moscow. There was a time when it was not true. There may come a time when it will not be true. The earth revolves around the sun once a year. There was a time when it did not revolve, and there may be a time when it will not revolve. Such truths are called contingent; not because they are not subject to uniform laws, but to distinguish them from necessary truths.

The whole is greater than its part, is a true proposition, necessarily true. That it should not be true is an impossibility. There is no such impossibility attaching to propositions affirming contingent truth.

The truths of geometry are necessary truths. That all right angles are equal, always was and always will be true, everywhere.

How can contingent truths be distinguished from necessary truths? Some writers state the marks of necessary truths, such as absolute certainty, and the fact that the opposite of a necessary truth is not only false but absurd. These are facts respecting necessary truths; but we do not look at these facts and infer from them that the truth is a necessary one. We distinguish between contingent and necessary truths by direct seeing. When we cognize a contingent truth, we cognize it as contingent; when we cognize a necessary truth, we cognize it as necessary: just as when we cognize a white object, we cognize it as white, and when we cognize a black object, we cognize it as black. Some contingent truths are cognized directly and some indirectly; the same is true of necessary truths.

Some writers refer contingent truths to the understanding, and necessary truths to the reason. It is the mind which distinguishes contingent from necessary truths, not certain imaginary entities called understanding and reason.

The distinction between the understanding and reason, to which so great importance is attached by some, is simply the distinction between contingent and necessary truth—a distinction by no means of modern discovery, as is well known to those who are at all acquainted with the earlier English writers on morals and theology.

Some writers seem to teach that necessary truths, or the truths of reason, are more intimately connected with the mind than contingent truths—truths of the understanding. They use language which implies that some necessary truths are native to the mind, and are evolved from it on certain occasions.

There is no reason to think that any truth is native to the mind in any other sense than that the mind has capacity to cognize it. The relation of the mind to all kinds of truth is the same. The mind cognizes, truth is cognized. No truths are evolved from the mind except as the mind is the object of cognition.

It is commonly supposed that greater certainty attaches to necessary than to contingent truths. All necessary truths are certain, absolutely certain. But all contingent truths are not therefore void of certainty. A contingent truth may be as certain as a necessary truth. It is certain that there is such a place as London. It is certain that Washington lived. We are as certain of the truth of these propositions as we are of the proposition which affirms the equality of alternate angles.

All necessary truths are certain. Some contingent truths are certain, and some are doubtful. The uncertainty of a truth has reference to our cognizing power, not to the truth itself. If it be a truth, if the proposition is true, it is certainly true.

Another distinction of importance is that between intuitive and deductive truths. Intuitive truths are also called self-evident truths. Some writers seem to regard intuitive truths as coming from the mind, whereas they come from the mind only in the sense that they are cognized by the mind. Intuitive truths do not constitute a class of truths generically different from other truths, as geometrical differ from geological truths. The term intuitive has reference to the mode of cognition, not to the nature of the truths. Intuitive truths are those which are cognized directly, immediately, without the aid of any other truths. In every department of knowledge there are some truths that are self-evident—which are cognized intuitively. Our intuitions are not inspirations— knowledge derived from a source differing from that whence our other knowledge is derived. They are direct cognitions of the mind. They are native only as our cognizing capacity is native.

Deductive truths are those cognized by the aid of other truths. The term would indicate that all truths mediately cognized were wrapped up in self-evident truths, and deduced from them. Some truths are deduced from other truths; but some truths are seen to be true in conseqence of our having seen certain other truths to be true. These cannot properly be said to be deduced from those truths, certainly not in the sense of being evolved from them. Inferential would perhaps be a better term than deductive. All our cognitions are either intuitive or inferential. We infer that a proposition is true, that is, discern its truth, in consequence of having discerned the truth of some other proposition or propositions.

If a man denies intuitive truths, he cannot be reasoned with. He denies every thing. It does not follow from this, that all inferential truths are educed from intuitive truths. We perceive some things to be true because we have intuitively cognized some other things to be true.

What truths have we a right to regard as intuitive? May every man have a set of intuitions of his own? When he wishes a thing to be true and cannot prove it, may he place it among his intuitions? Certainly not. Those truths only can be regarded as intuitive which are received as true by all men. Intuitive truths are admitted either by word or deed by all men.

Faith and Reason.—The relation of faith to reason is a very simple one. They are not antagonistic, but concordant. Faith is confidence in testimony, which involves confidence in character. Testimony is a source of knowledge. The knowledge of a jury respecting the guilt or innocence of a prisoner is from testimony.

Testimony may give us certain knowledge. Only a few Americans have seen the city of Canton, yet all

Americans are sure there is such a city. This certain knowledge rests upon testimony alone. It is reasonable for a man to believe good testimony; that is, it is reasonable to have faith.

Religious and secular faith differ only as their objects differ. The doctrines of Revelation are received by faith—that is, on the testimony of God. It is certainly reasonable to believe God's testimony; therefore it is reasonable to exercise religious faith. There is, therefore, no antagonism between religious faith and reason.

If we have God's testimony, it is reasonable to believe it, whether we can fully understand it or not. To believe that which we do not comprehend, is not to believe that which is unreasonable and absurd.

We must have satisfactory evidence that we have God's testimony. We must examine the evidence on which the claim of the Bible to be the testimony of God rests. If we find satisfactory evidence, the Bible is to be believed.

It may be asked, Suppose it contain contradictions and absurdities, are they to be believed? Certainly not. If it contain contradictions and absurdities, and it is certain that they are not interpolations, then there is not satisfactory evidence that it is God's testimony; for his testimony cannot be contradictory and absurd. The alleged contradictions must be disposed of in considering the evidence of the Bible's being God's testimony. If the conclusion be that the

Bible is God's word, it is reasonable to believe all it contains. Faith, confidence in His testimony and character, is in the highest degree reasonable.

The Infinite.—There is no such thing as a general infinite. There are infinite things or attributes, just as there are true propositions; but the infinite and the true are not independent entities. We cognize infinite objects, and can thus form an abstract idea of infinity. The idea is not definable. As we say truth is that in which all true propositions agree, so we may say that the infinite is that in which all infinite objects agree.

That is infinite which has no limit. That which we cognize as limitless is to us infinite. We must distinguish between the infinite and the indefinite. God's wisdom is infinite; it transcends all our powers of apprehension. So of His mercy and His benevolence. Infinite existence is everlasting existence. When we speak of God as the infinite existence, we mean that all His attributes are infinite.

The human mind can form no adequate apprehension of the infinite—that is, of infinite things. And yet it is not, properly speaking, a negative apprehension which we have of it. The fact that we cannot know every thing about a subject or object, does not prove that we cannot know any thing about it. The fact that we cannot by searching find out God to perfection, does not prove that we cannot know many things respecting Him.

God is infinite; that is, His existence and attributes are without limit—transcend all our powers of apprehension. We know that nothing can be added to them.

There has been a great deal written about the absolute and infinite which conveys no meaning to such as have not the faculty of understanding the unintelligible. Many assertions have been made for which there is no proof. For example, Mansel says: "That which is conceived as absolute and infinite, must be conceived of as containing within itself the sum, not only of all actual, but of all possible modes of being."

"The nature of man's conviction in regard to infinity," says McCosh, "is fitted to impress us, at one and the same time, with the strength and the weakness of human intelligence, which is powerful in that it can apprehend so much, but feeble in that it can apprehend no more. The idea entertained is felt to be inadequate, but this is one of its excellences, that it is felt to be inadequate; for it would indeed be lamentably deficient, if it did not acknowledge of itself that it falls infinitely beneath the magnitude of the object. The mind is led by an inward tendency to stretch its ideas wider and wider, but is made to know, at the most extreme point which it has reached, that there is something further on. It is thus impelled to be ever striving after something which it has not yet reached, and to look beyond the limits of time into eternity beyond, in which there is the prospect of a noble occupation in beholding, through ages which can come to no end, and a space which has no bounds, the manifestation of a might and an excellence of which we can never know all, but of which we may ever know more. It is an idea which would ever allure us up toward a God of infinite perfection, and yet make us feel more and more impressively the higher we ascend, that we are, after all, infinitely beneath Him. Man's capacity to form such an idea is a proof that he was formed by an infinite God, and in the image of an infinite God; his incapacity in spite of all his efforts to form a higher idea, is fitted to show us how wide the space and how impassable the gulf which separates man as finite from God the infinite."

THE END.

ENGLISH LANGUAGE.

Exposition of the Grammatical Structure of the English Language.
By JOHN MULLIGAN, A. M. Large 12mo, 574 pages.

This work is a complete system of English Grammar, embracing not only all that has been developed by the later philologists, but also the results of years of study on the part of its author. One great advantage of this book is its admirable arrangement. Instead of proceeding at once to the dry details which are distasteful to the pupil, Mr. M. commences by viewing the sentence as a whole, analyzing it into its proper parts, and exhibiting their connection; and, after having thus parsed the sentence logically, proceeds to consider the individual words which compose it, in all their grammatical relations.

Dictionary of the English Language.
By ALEXANDER REED, A. M. 12mo, 572 pages.

This work, which is designed for schools, has been compiled with direct reference to their wants, by a teacher of experience, judgment, and scholarship. It contains, in small compass and the most convenient form, the Pronunciation and Definitions of all English words authorized by good usage; a full Vocabulary of Foreign Roots; an accented list of Greek, Latin, and Scripture Proper Names; and an Appendix, showing the pronunciation of nearly three thousand of the most important Geographical Names. It is philosophical in its arrangement, grouping derivatives under their primitives, and gives the root of every word in the language, thus affording a clear insight into comparative philology.

Either as a work of reference, or a text-book for daily study, this Dictionary will be found to possess important advantages over all others. Some of our best scholars commend it in the strongest terms: among whom may be mentined Rev. Dr. HENRY, late of New York University; D. M. REESE, formerly Superintendent of Schools of New York; and the late Bishop WAINWRIGHT. Prof. FROST, of Philadelphia, pronounces the plan excellent. Rev. M. P. PARKS, late Prof. U. S. Military Academy at West Point, says: "I consider it superior to any of the School Dictionaries with which I am acquainted."

D. APPLETON & CO.'S PUBLICATIONS.

The Hand-Book of Household Science.

A Popular Account of Heat, Light, Air, Aliment, and Cleansing, in their Scientific Principles and Domestic Applications. By E. L. YOUMANS, M.D. 12mo, Illustrated, 470 pages.

Various books have been prepared which cross the field of domestic science at different points, but this is the first work that traverses and occupies the whole ground. Hardly a page can be opened to that does not convey information interesting and valuable to every person who dwells in a house. The work will be found not only of high practical utility, but captivating to the student, and unequalled in the interest of its recitations.

From the Superintendent of Public Instruction in the State of Pennsylvania.
"The daily and hourly importance of the topics embraced in the work, their imperious claims upon public attention, and their intimate connection with individual and social welfare, together with the compendious arrangement and copious fulness of information presented, and the cautious accuracy and precision of statement, make it a publication of the highest practical value for both the household and the school.
"Very respectfully yours,
"Prof. EDWARD L. YOUMANS. HENRY C. HICKOK."

From the Superintendent of Schools of the State of New York.
"It embodies scientific information of the highest importance, arranged with much care, and so clearly stated that even the ordinary mind can scarcely fail to grasp and retain the truths it unfolds and illustrates. It would prove a most valuable class-book in our high schools, and I am satisfied that an examination into its merits would result in its general introduction into such institutions. Very respectfully yours,
"H. H. VAN DYCK, Superintendent Public Instruction."

From the Springfield Republican.
"It is the work of a man thoroughly scientific and thorougly practical. It is no extravagance to say that a mastery of its contents will secure a better knowledge of the applications of Chemistry, Physiology, and Natural Philosophy, to life and life's concerns, than the combined treatises upon these subjects which are usually found in our school-rooms."

From the Detroit Advertiser.
"This is one of the most valuable and important books that has of late been issued from the press. It will do more to elevate and connect the ordinary duties of household life with the domain of science than any other work yet published. It is so arranged that the general reader and the man of science may refer to it with satisfaction; but it is also a book which ought by all means to be introduced in our schools, and which every young woman who expects to be any thing more than a doll or parlor automaton, should study and become as familiar with as she is with her prayer-book."

From the Philadelphia Saturday Courier.
"Few persons realize—few persons begin to realize—the importance of thoroughly understanding the nature and effects of light, heat, air, and food; yet the value of such knowledge can hardly be overstated. Mr. Youmans' work is the clearest and fullest exposition of science in those relations that has yet appeared. School committees and persons directly interested in education, who have long been searching for a work of this kind, will rejoice to find the fruit of their quest in this manual. It is a valuable book, written for a valuable purpose: the desire to lift our ordinary domestic life into the dignity of intelligence pervades it throughout, and tinctures it in the grain."

D. APPLETON & CO.'S PUBLICATIONS.

THE
Correlation and Conservation of Forces.
WITH AN
INTRODUCTION AND BRIEF BIOGRAPHICAL NOTICES.

By EDWARD L. YOUMANS, M.D. 12mo, 490 pages.

CONTENTS.

I. By W. R. GROVE. The Correlation of Physical Forces.
II. By Prof. HELMHOLTZ. The Interaction of Natural Forces.
III. By J. R. MAYER. 1. Remarks on the Forces of Inorganic Nature.
2. On Celestial Dynamics.
3. On the Mechanical Equivalent of Heat.
IV. By Dr. FARADAY. Some Thoughts on the Conservation of Forces.
V. By Prof. LIEBIG. The Connection and Equivalence of Forces.
VI. By Dr. CARPENTER. The Correlation of the Physical and Vital Forces.

"This work is a very welcome addition to our scientific literature, and will be particularly acceptable to those who wish to obtain a popular, but at the same time precise and clear view of what Faraday justly calls the highest law in physical science, the principle of the conservation of force. Sufficient attention has not been paid to the publication of collected monographs or memoirs upon special subjects. Dr. Youmans' work exhibits the value of such collections in a very striking manner, and we earnestly hope his excellent example may be followed in other branches of science."—*American Journal of Science.*

"It was a happy thought which suggested the publication of this volume. The question is often asked, and not so easily answered, What are the new doctrines of the Correlation and Conservation of Forces? In this volume we have the answer, and with the reasons of its chief expounders; those who are ignorant on that theme, can thus question the original authorities."—*New Englander.*

"We here have the original expositions of the new Philosophy of Forces, accompanied by an excellent exposition of both the expositions and the expositors; the whole will be a rare treat to the lovers of advancing scientific thought."—*Methodist Quarterly Review.*

"This is, perhaps, the most remarkable book of the age. We have here the latest discoveries, and the highest results of thought concerning the nature, laws, and connections of the forces of the universe. No higher or more sublime problem can engage the intellect of man than is discussed by these doctors of science intent alone on arriving at the truth."—*Detroit Free Press.*

"This work presents a praiseworthy specimen of complete and faithful authorship, and its publication at this time will form an epoch in the experience of many thinking minds."— *ibune.*

ENGLISH LANGUAGE

Hand-Book of the English Language.

By G. R. LATHAM, M.D., F.R.S. 12mo, 398 pages.

The ethnological relations of the English Language, its history and analysis, its spelling and pronunciation, etymology and syntax, are here treated with a completeness, learning, and grasp of intellect, that will be vainly sought elsewhere. The elements of our tongue, the successive changes by which it has been modified, the origin of its peculiar expressions, and other subjects of like importance and interest, receive due attention of the author, who ranks among the most accomplished scholars of England. Whether for private study, or as a manual for college and high-school classes, Dr. Latham's Hand-Book will be found one of the most useful works extant in the department of belles-lettres.

Graham's English Synonymes,

Classified and explained; with practical exercises, designed for schools and private tuition; with an introduction and illustrative authorities. By HENRY REED, LL.D. 12mo, 344 pages.

This treatise is intended to teach the right use of words. It explains the principal synonymes of the language, classified and arranged in pairs, and illustrates their use at different eras with passages from Shakespeare, Milton, and Wordsworth. Exercises are appended, which require the pupil to fill blanks by the insertion of the words compared, selecting in each case the one that is adapted to the context. Thus practically impressed on the pupil's mind, their distinctive meanings will not soon be forgotten.

The attention of teachers is particularly invited to this work, as one of the most useful that can be found for imparting a thorough acquaintance with our tongue. Besides teaching the student how to avoid common inaccuracies of expression, and training him to that precision which is essential to a good style, it will be found highly serviceable in disciplining his mind by accustoming it to a critical appreciation of nice distinctions. Wherever it has been introduced into academic or collegiate institutions, it has awakened great interest in the study of words, and proved a valuable auxiliary to courses of grammar and rhetoric.

History of English Literature.

By WILLIAM SPALDING, A.M., Professor of Logic, Rhetoric, and Metaphysics, in the University of St. Andrews. 12mo, 413 pages.

The above work is offered as a Text-book for the use of advanced Schools and Academies. It traces the literary progress of the nation from Anglo-Saxon times to the present day, and furnishes a comprehensive outline of the origin and growth of our language. Those literary monuments of early date which are thought most worthy of attention, are described with considerable fulness and in an attractive manner. Constant effort is made to arouse reflection, both by occasional remarks on the relations between intellectual culture and the world of reality and action, and by hints as to the laws on which criticism is founded. The characteristics of the most celebrated modern works are analyzed at length.

The style of the author is remarkably clear and interesting, compelling the reader to linger over his pages with unwearied attention.

Manual of Grecian and Roman Antiquities.

By Dr. E. F. BOJESEN, with Notes and Questions by Rev. THOMAS K. ARNOLD. 12mo, 209 pages.

The present Manuals of Greek and Roman Antiquities are far superior to any thing on the same topics as yet offered to the American public. A leading Review of Germany says of the Roman Manual:—"Small as the compass of it is, we may confidently affirm that it is a great improvement on all preceding works of the kind. We no longer meet with the wretched old method, in which subjects essentially distinct are herded together, and connected subjects disconnected, but have a simple, systematic arrangement, by which the reader readily receives a clear representation of Roman life. We no longer stumble against countless errors in detail, which, though long ago assailed and extirpated by Niebuhr and others, have found their last place of refuge in our manuals. The recent investigations of philologists and jurists have been extensively, but carefully and circumspectly used."

Elements of Logic.

With an Introductory view of Philosophy in general, and a Preliminary View of the Reason. By HENRY W. TAPPAN. 12mo, 467 pages.

Not considering Logic as an abstraction, Prof. Tappan assigns it its proper place among kindred sciences, and takes the student over the whole field of Philosophy, that the connection of its various parts may be distinctly perceived. He presents the subject, not merely as a method of obtaining inferences from truths, but also as a method of establishing those first truths and general principles that must precede all deduction. The great starting-points of theory, the sources to which we must look for premises in every department of science, are viewed in connection with Logic; the relations between the two are examined; and the proper understanding of both is thus greatly facilitated. This is new ground; yet it is what the profound thinker and all who would master the subject have long needed.

In carrying out this plan, the author begins with Philosophy in general; shows the distinction between the Phenomenal and the Metaphenomenal, the Objective and the Subjective, the Sensual and the Transcendental; defines Ideas and the laws of their development; and then proceeds to treat of the divisions of General Philosophy, Metaphysics, and Nomology—in the latter of which, with Ethics, Æsthetics, and Somatology, Logic is included.

The interesting questions incidentally opened up, such as the Criteria of a True Philosophy, receive attention, and then, after a brief preliminary view of the Reason and its functions, we are introduced to Logic Proper. The evolution of Ideas, in all their variety, is first set forth at length; and numerous important points, now for the first time found in a system of Logic, such as the relation between matter and spirit, right and wrong, freedom and responsibility, are discussed in a manner which proves the author a practical adept in the science he would teach. Inductive and Deductive Logic follow; the latter of which embraces all the rules, principles, and formulæ to be found in the text-books of former dialecticians, and to which, for the most part, they confine themselves.

The work closes with a masterly dissertation on the nature of proof, its different kinds, degrees of evidence, circumstantial evidence, reasoning from experience and analogy, and the calculation of chances. Important as these subjects are, and intimately as they are connected with the work of the dialectician, they have heretofore had no place in treatises on Logic; Mr. Tappen is the first to unfold their connection with this science, and the clearness and comprehensiveness with which he has treated them leave nothing to be desired.

www.ingramcontent.com/pod-product-compliance
Lightning Source LLC
Chambersburg PA
CBHW030820230426
43667CB00008B/1299